Remember Who You Are!

How Family Values Can Influence Your Financial Goals

Bobby Dye

Dye Resource Management, LLC

RIDGELAND, MISSISSIPPI

Bobby Dye/Dye Resource Management, LLC
1062 Highland Colony Parkway, Suite 225
Ridgeland, MS 39157
www.dyefinancial.net

Book Layout ©2013 BookDesignTemplates.com

Ordering Information:
Quantity sales. Special discounts are available on quantity purchases by corporations, associations, and others. For details, contact the "Special Sales Department" at the address above.

Bobby Dye/Remember Who You Are! —1st ed.
ISBN 9798393681623

Credit for the painting on the cover of this book goes to my daughter, Laura. It was inspired by this picture my wife, Darnell, took of me (on the left), my dad Spence, and my son Gary. She also took a picture from behind us, showing the Country Club of Jackson, Mississippi, where we spent countless hours together as three generations enjoying many rounds of golf. On a few occasions, my mother's father joined us, and FOUR generations played a few rounds.

When Darnell took these pictures, she said, "I don't know why it came to my mind to do this, but the three of you will thank me. This will be something special one day!"

She was right.

Contents

Dye Resource
Management
LLC

"But they who wait for the Lord shall renew
Their strength; they shall mount up with wings
Like eagles; they shall run and not be weary;
They shall walk and not faint."
–   Isaiah 46:3

"I believe God made me for a purpose, but he also made me
fast. And when I run, I feel his pleasure."
–   Eric Liddell, Chariots of Fire

In Dedication to

The memory of my mom and dad; my grandparents on both sides of the family; my nephew, Jake Kramer; my uncle, Gary Gliessner; and the multiple generations before me that helped "clear the trail" a century or more ahead of me that made my path a lot easier.

I am proud to be a Dye, and I am indebted to the values you passed on to me.

You will not be forgotten as your blood runs through my veins and multiple generations to follow.

Foreword

Before sitting down to write a book, you first must nail down the direction you would like to go.

My initial thought was to write about myself and the experiences I've enjoyed during my life of sixty-plus years, but then I started thinking about how much I've been influenced by my multigenerational family. They've given me more than enough blessings to fill a book, and I believe the lessons they've taught me over the years can be useful for anyone who picks up this book.

In the chapters that follow, you'll get to know some of the people who served as the cornerstones of the Dye family name. I hope their stories are as helpful for you as they have been for me.

When it comes to telling our family's story, there's no better place to start than Grammaw Dye. She was a godly woman who prayed every day on her knees on the dirt floors of her home for her children and the generations of children to come.

She influenced my becoming a Christian during my senior year in college, so she obviously had a huge impact on my life. The Lord used her to bring about change in my life, particularly after the death of her husband and my Grampa.

Although her words were simple and unassuming, they were strong, which garnered my love and respect for her even more.

The title of this book is *Remember Who You Are!* because that is what my grandmother would tell her children as they went out on the town. She knew they would be embarrassed because they were dirt poor, but she would say to them, "When you leave this house, remember who you are—you represent this family."

Then there's my mom's father, Carl "PaPa" Gliessner, who was also an instrumental part of my life. PaPa was a hero—a man revered by many people for his quiet strength and strong character and a man of his word.

He was the man I was most compared to by my mother. She always said I was like her father, and I always took that as a great compliment.

My father, Spence Dye, saw PaPa as his role model too. He said that when he had lived his life in full, he wanted to be as respected in life as his father-in-law. I always told my father that he not only met that goal but exceeded it—and that was a tall order.

I have had many goals in life, but two of my of my lifelong goals stand out in my mind as the most difficult, if not impossible.

The first is a goal I set when I was starting my career as a twenty-one-year-old. I determined then that I want to go as far in life—from where I started to where I ultimately end up—as my father did. That was an extremely lofty goal because, as you'll read in Chapter 1, he was an incredible success story who accomplished a lot, not only as a businessman but as a human being—a father, husband, and family man.

I have the rest of my life to chase that goal, and while I consider it nearly impossible, it still drives me. It is an honor, not an obligation.

The other goal I set, unfortunately, *is* impossible. I wanted to be able to fully repay my mother for everything she did for me. Even if I spent every hour and every minute, of every day for the rest of my life, I could never pay her back for all that she did for me.

Sadly, she has passed away now. It was a goal I would have never been able to achieve anyhow, but it was something I wish I could have done. She always deserved my best; she always gave me hers.

So, I want you to know, this book is not about me. It is not to build me up or to do anything other than shed light on the many blessings my family has given me.

Everyone in my family is close to me, from my wife, children, brother and sister, to my nieces and nephews. We are a family of helpers. As you will soon read, we did not have much growing up, but we did have a love for each other, a caring heart for strangers, and a genuine willingness to help.

Why? Because we understand and have faced financial struggles of our own. My parents, especially my father, had nothing growing up. He was a big giver, which was so ironic because usually when you give things away, it means you have plenty to give.

He gave everything he had to everybody.

We have never been a family to ask for help. We just did it for ourselves, but we were always reaching out to help other people. We enjoyed it. It's how we were raised.

If nothing else, what I really want people to understand is that there are people who still care. I care, and I care about you, but I do not care if you have $10 million or one penny. While my family is blessed enough to be financially stable now, that wasn't always the case.

I have a wonderful wife, Darnell, who has always supported me. In the tough times, she walked beside me and never complained. She always encouraged me and pushed me to do better, and when I succeeded, she shared in my excitement.

She always trusted in my doing it "my way," and she understood that it takes a significant amount of time to build a business the right way. There are no shortcuts to success.

Our greatest blessings of all are our two children: our daughter, Laura, and her husband, Andrew Hogin; and son, Gary and his wife, Shelby Dye.

I teach my children the same thing Grammaw Dye taught her kids years ago: "Remember who you are. Don't forget that you represent the whole family."

So, as you read this book, just remember it is about family. It is about the people who surround us. It is about being on a team where the players give it their all.

All these things make us who we are and who we strive to be for our clients.

CHAPTER 1

A Father's Legacy

This is an American story more than a century in the making.

It is the story of one family's rise from rags to riches—the building of their legacy toward intergenerational knowledge and wisdom regarding money.

It is a story of how one family makes the lives better for the generations who follow them. It is also about the values each continues to pass on.

It could potentially be your story, too.

This first chapter was written by my dad in 1987, a narration of my family's history that was never published and I am happy to share for the first time here.

As Written by Spence Dye in 1987

For the past several years, I have been thinking about writing the story of my life. I have put it off, both because of being self-conscious about it, and because I'm not even sure I know how to do it well enough to make it worth anything to anyone who might read it in a few years.

There are a number of reasons why I am finally starting out to put forth an effort to talk about my life from 1926 until the end of 1987.

The dominant factor, I think, is that I hope my great-grandchildren will have an interest in knowing where they came from and what I saw and experienced and felt during my life—and try to relate to that. Another reason, and one I think is most important, is that someone might be interested in knowing what life was like to a generation that lived through a transitional period of gigantic development from the horse and buggy days to the landing of people on the moon and beyond.

I am still amazed at what happened in this country with the technological changes that have taken place in my sixty-two years. We have developed from a society of youth where we went "to town" once or twice a month in a springboard wagon to an era where two cars, three TV sets, VCR, and a video camcorder in many homes are commonplace. If future generations make this kind of technological progress, the world will be an exciting place to live in and survive.

I know that a more subtle, but very real, reason for putting whatever I'm doing down on paper is because of personal ego. I hate to think that all this pride I have in what little success I have gained will simply go down the drain when I die. I want someone to know that I was down here for a time and lived a life that was fun and exciting and maybe a little worthwhile. Wrapped up in that, too, is a love for my country and family that is absolutely boundless. If all of these can be expressed to any degree, then what I'm trying to do may be worth something to my family members who are yet to come. At the very least, I hope some future family member will say, "I'm glad he wrote this because it helps me know myself a little better."

I don't know an awful lot about my family and where they came from. All I know about my Dad's side of the family is that he was orphaned at an early age and was raised by an uncle in Malden, Missouri. As good and loyal Southerners, I remember we were all ashamed over the fact that his father was a hated Yankee soldier that met and married his mother in Chickamauga, Tennessee after the War of Northern Aggression. I must say, none of our family ever spoke of or asked about our grandfather after we learned that he was a Yankee soldier from Illinois that fought in the Battle of Chickamauga and later married my grandmother.

They subsequently had six children with my father being the youngest. He was about four years of age when they both died and he was raised by an uncle, Jim Dye, in Malden, Missouri.

It was in Malden that my dad, at twenty-one, married my mother, Nina Dale Taylor, who was only sixteen years of age. Six children were born to them while they lived and worked as sharecroppers in Malden. How in the world they survived would be an incredible story, if it could have been told.

In 1924, my Dad got an opportunity to move to a 100-acre plot of land just outside of Leachville, Arkansas, on a sharecrop program. He moved his young family in a wagon pulled by a team of Missouri mules. Two years later, I was born. And, in 1931, my baby brother, Charles Brent, arrived. With that meager background, I will give the snapshots of my life as I recall them.

1926 – 1937

The area around Leachville was cotton country, and the land was rich and black.

We had a little land that we sharecropped, and my earliest memories are getting to ride to the cotton gin on top of a wagon filled with cotton and pulled by two strapping Missouri mules.

I never have understood why they were called Missouri mules, but that was what everyone referred to them as, even though they were bred and foaled in Arkansas.

My dad, Charlie Dye, was one of the most gentle people I have ever known. By September of 1931, when the last of our family (Charles) was born, he was a father of eight small children. Eight children by the time he was only thirty-nine years of age. It was a heavy burden to put on the back of a dirt-poor sharecropper.

I never saw him lay a belt or a switch on any one of us, even though his patience had to wear thin at times. Yet, even during the hardest times, I can remember that he always kept a good sense of humor and he always laughed hardest when one of his kids said or did something. That sense of humor stayed with him all of his life.

Nina Dale, our mother, also was a person with a great sense of humor and a love for her family that was unfailing no matter what. However, she had an even deeper sense that mandated strong family discipline. She always kept a willow switch on top of the old wood cookstove and could swing it harder and straighter than Jack Nicklaus can hit a two-iron.

When Mama said, "that's enough now," we all knew that it was time to halt whatever we were doing.

Mama was our strength, always. If I heard, "we may be poor but we are proud," once in my life, I heard it a million times. As we grew up and became old enough to go out, she always would say, "Remember who you are," as if we had a name, fame, and wealth that needed to be guarded and upheld.

It worked, though, because it gave us a sense of pride that couldn't be supported by the conditions of our life.

The little old shack that I was born in was smack dab in the middle of a cotton patch just outside of Leachville, Arkansas. It had two sleeping rooms, a living room, and a kitchen. I used to jokingly say that I didn't know what it was like to sleep alone until I got married. We had a double bed in the living room where Mom and Dad slept. My two sisters, Evelyn and Freda, had the privilege of having one bedroom all to themselves while six boys crammed into the other room.

If you don't think that wasn't an ordeal, try to imagine that happening today.

We didn't even own a radio back then, and even if we had, there wasn't a transmitting station to get a signal. We did have a wind-up Victrola and owned two records that we played so much you could barely tell what Jimmy Rogers was singing.

There was good music available, however, if you like good fiddle and guitar playing. In the early 1930s, a local group of neighbor boys would come to our house and we would put the furniture out on the porch and our neighbors would come over to that old shack and would rock it off the foundation. Dad always made homebrew and our place was pretty popular with kinfolks and neighbors when it was time to party.

We were always proud that one young fiddle player by the name of Wade Ray played at our house. He was an excellent fiddler and later played in St. Louis over KMOX on the Saturday Night Hayride. Locally, the group back then was called the "Linger Longer Night Hawks" and they became a very popular country music band around that part of the country. My mother's half-brother, Floyd Dismukes, played the piano with them, and we always thought Uncle Floyd was our claim to fame.

The Great Depression

When the depression hit in the early 30s, we never felt it. When you are eating milk gravy and side meat for breakfast and navy beans for what we called dinner and supper with cornbread and buttermilk, it is kind of hard to go downhill with a depression.

However, cotton hit rock bottom, so we were kicked off of the land we had been allowed to use for sharecropping. A huge landowner called the B.C. Land Company offered my dad $4 an acre to clear some new ground and he accepted the offer. My dad and three older brothers operated two cross-cut saws while my brother Max and I trimmed the trees and stacked brush.

The land company allowed us to take enough trees to the sawmill to build us a small house on the banks of an irrigation ditch, so we would have something to live in. That green lumber dried out when hot weather came, and the cracks were wide enough to put your fingers through. I remember very distinctly being able to see through the cracks in the floor and counting the chickens that bedded down under the house.

When our first winter came in this shack, we got a lot of cardboard and newspapers and tacked those up as best we could. It helped some. But on those cold, winter nights you can bet that it helped sleeping three to a bed. We always kidded and laughed about having a central heating system. We had a wood stove for heating right in the center of the house and we kept it going night and day. At least we had an inexhaustible supply of wood!

Just down the ditch from where we lived was an old dirt-floored hut where an elderly widow lived in alone.

As poor as we were, we all worried about her.

She had a few chickens and eight billy goats that lived in her place—about as much in as they lived outside. Her place was totally filthy, and she looked as if she had never had a bath in her entire life. If she had family, they never came for a visit. All of us kids felt sorry for her and tried to help her as much as we could.

Mama seemed to preach to us more than ever the importance of staying clean. We all had to take a bath at least once a week in that Number 3 washtub that we used. As repugnant as that sounds, taking a bath in a washtub when the temperature outside is zero or below and not much warmer inside is an ordeal you need to endure to appreciate. However, if that repels you, the fact that at least two of us would bathe in the same tub of water will make it even worse.

The following spring of 1935, the Depression had deepened, and things were going from bad to worse.

Our diet was so inadequate that I, and a couple of my brothers, had several sores on our legs and arms. We couldn't afford to go to the doctor, so Mama made up a kind of Calumine potion to put on to dry up the sores. Also, she started buying apples and other fruits to improve our diet. It worked because the sores dried up, leaving scars that stayed with me for years.

Mom and Dad appeared to be more desperate during this time than I care to remember.

The three older boys were growing up and I'm sure they recognized that change of any kind would be an improvement. My sister, Freda, who was about ten years old, caught spinal meningitis and died. I don't remember too many of the details, but I do know that the lack of medical facilities and knowledge in that part of the country killed her chance for survival. It left us with six boys and one sister. From that moment on, my sister Evelyn was extra special to me, and I think to my brothers, too.

Anyway, due to the sorry situation we were in and the insistence of Grandma Dismukes, Mama's mother, we moved into town. No one had a job, so we were lucky to find an old shotgun house to move into. My Grandmother Dismukes lived in town with her husband, Will Dismukes, who was the town constable. When my real grandfather died, Grandma met Will Dismukes and they had a good life together. They had a son, Floyd Dismukes, that was my first role model for what I wanted to be when I grew up. He could play the piano, was tall and good looking, and always wore clean clothes. He also played tennis—which I admired even though I didn't really know what that meant.

He made his living working at the local, and only, funeral home in Leachville. When they let him drive the ambulance, we thought he was the hottest shot in town. Needless to say, he was quite a playboy and he thoroughly enjoyed life. He loved playing with the ladies and tipping the jug on Saturday nights and quite a bit in between. My mother adored him as her baby brother, and we all thought he deserved it.

Mama also had a full brother, Burke Taylor, who lived in town. Uncle Burke worked at the compress in town and was the general supervisor of that operation. Uncle Burke was intelligent, hardworking, and sober, always. If he ever took a drink of liquor in his life, I never heard about it. I know that I loved him always and whenever he told me to do something, I never hesitated a moment. Where Uncle Floyd had flair and charm that appealed to almost everyone, Uncle Burke had quiet, solid strength that could pull you through anything.

My Grandma, Evalina Dixie Giles Taylor Dismukes, was literally the most elegant and gracious lady I have ever known. Grandma always stood very straight with her head held high, and even when I was seven or eight years old, I knew that she had passed on something special from her genes. My admiration and adoration must have shown because I became her favorite. Part of that special feeling from her may have been caused by the fact that I was named after

Spence Mike Taylor, and partly because she always said I was the spitting image of my grandpa.

Whatever the reason, I loved it and took every possible advantage of it.

The transition in lifestyles from living in the country where we saw very few people to living in town where there was constant people activity was hard to get used to. From the very first, I loved every minute of it. My brother, Max, only a year and nine months older than me, and I were pretty good friends, so we were able to hold our own meeting other boys our age that lived in town. It sure did help that Max was built a lot bigger than most other kids his age and was always a good athlete. It certainly discouraged the bullies that are a part of every boy population and helped to accelerate our acceptance of the town gang.

Our family was about as close during this time as close can get. In a sense, we were two families, with Harlan, Vane, and Tom in the role of the three older boys and Max, me, and Brent being the little ones. My sister, Evelyn, had a special place in the family that was well deserved for a lot of reasons.

She was pretty with a sparkling personality and innate class that stood out all on it's own. Harlan and Vane were very close being the two oldest and pretty much stuck together in local activities and found it hard to include Tom too much because of the age difference. The same held true with Max and me in our treatment of Brent. He was five years younger than me so there was no way we could establish comradeship in those early years.

I think we all took to living in town right off and life really began to become exciting for all of us. My mother took in washing and did some housework for people in town. Dad killed some hogs and sold meat from door to door off of a wagon pulled by a team of mules for a while, and the older boys did odd jobs when they could be found. There wasn't much money, and we still ate a lot of milk gravy and fried baloney (bologna), and I learned to tolerate "Poke salad" since it grew wild and was free. That may sound a little absurd, but it really is true.

Living near my grandmother was a unique experience for me. We developed a special relationship, and I loved her very much. In about 1936, Grandpa Dismukes died, and she lived along the edge of town. I spent a lot of days and nights at her house. She gave me the motivation to "be somebody." She believed in reading. She had a wall of books that included a complete set of encyclopedias, the "Hardy Boys" series, "Little Women," "Ben-Hur," and a series of books on "The War Between The States" and a family Bible.

Grandma insisted that I read, read, and read some more. She also talked a lot about how the Yankees invaded Tennessee during the Civil War and that Northerners were just a different kind of people. She taught me that being a Southerner was a privilege and that being a Christian was as essential as breathing. While most of that didn't mean anything at the time, it surely did provide seed for a conscience that stayed with me always.

In the little over two years that we lived in town, we lived in four different houses that I can remember. We moved so much that we used to kid about how every time we walked out into the backyard, the hens would lay down and cross their legs so they could be tied and loaded up and ready to move.

However, we now had electricity in the house and this was a great improvement over trying to read by the light put out by those old kerosene lamps that we were used to using. We still had to get water from the pump in the backyard and the outside privy was still a part of our way of life. Life had eased up some, but Easy Street didn't come to our part of town.

The Depression by 1936 had gotten so bad that even people who owned property started to eat a little baloney and gravy. Those of us who had been poor all along pulled jokes on the newly arrived poverty group. We'd tell the boys learning to eat collard greens and poke salad to tie coal oil rags around their ankles to keep the cut worms from getting to them. Some of them were not too sure we were kidding.

Hope for many came with all the promises FDR (Franklin D. Roosevelt) made in his bid to become President. Everybody in the area believed in him, except my dad, and FDR won by a landslide. Dad always said "that man is going to take this country down" and I often thought he was the only Republican in Arkansas. If he wasn't alone, he sure didn't have much company.

Roosevelt bought in the "letters" system of government. The NRA (National Recovery Act), the CCC's (Civil Construction Corp.), the PWA (Public Works Administration), the WPA (Works Progress Administration), and some others I don't recall. My brother Vane joined the CCC and was gone from home for several months planting trees for the Corp, as it was called. Dad and Harlan got a job with the WPA, but the politics were pretty hard to take, and Dad could never get used to free handouts and playing politics for something he had no stomach for.

Max and I, meantime, found a secret to making a little change. A scrap place opened up in town that would buy iron, steel, aluminum, copper, zinc, and old rags. We took a little red wagon and found more junk to sell than anyone thought possible. This added a little change to help the budget and gave us the needed dime it took to get into the picture show house (movie theater) that had opened up in town.

In spite of all the hardships, I don't think I could have had a happier childhood. The love and togetherness in our family made for some great fun when everyone was home.

Luckily, there was great humor in our house and the pranks that were played kept everyone in a good mood. I learned early that it didn't pay to get mad at mealtime and refuse to eat. The first one that puckered up and refused to eat brought cheers from everyone else because they said it gave them more for themselves.

In 1936, when I was ten years old, a man in town gave me a job selling Grit magazines. I got a penny for every one I sold, and I learned a lot about the incentive plan in the free enterprise system. I must have shown a little promise because I got a cherished job of delivering the Sunday paper, and the pay was really good for this. It was a real thrill for me to be able to help out at home and have a little money for my own use.

In the spring of 1937, some of our neighbors moved to Michigan to work as fruit pickers in the huge orchards of southwest Michigan. They sent letters to Mom and Dad telling them the pay was good and that the growers were begging for workers. Our family immediately started making plans to go to Michigan. We bought a 1929 Whippet automobile, and that old jalopy was made ready for the trip. We took one-by-eight pieces of wood and bolted one on each side of the car to the running board. This created a well about seven inches deep. We used it to put our personal belongings for the trip north. The Whippet didn't have a trunk, so everything that we took with us had to be carried on top of the car and in those wells.

According to the plan, we would leave in May of 1937 and work through the peach crop and come back home to Leachville sometime in September. I could hardly wait to get started because I had never been to another town in my entire life. I couldn't wait to go through Manilla and Blytheville, Arkansas, and see for myself what I had been missing. Also, we had to cross the great Mississippi River at Cairo, Illinois where the Ohio and Mississippi join forces and that was just almost the greatest sight I could possibly imagine.

Finally, the day came for the trip North and the Whippet was fully packed and ready to go.

We had stored some of our belongings in Grandma's shed and the rest had been sold or given away.

The three older boys rode in the front seat with Mom, Dad, Sis, Max, Brent, and me in the back seat. After about twenty-five miles, most of the excitement had turned to the realization that this was going to be a real tough trip.

I don't remember too much about the trip except we drove the first day well until after dark and spent the night in a cheap tourist hotel for $3 a night. We were so worn out that we went to sleep immediately. Early the next day we made it through Kankakee, Champaign, and Urbana, Illinois and into Michigan. In the late afternoon, we found the farm near Baroda, Michigan where our friends were working, and our spirits were high.

The owner of the farm where our friends were living, and working was most receptive and hospitable to our family. He told us we were welcome to sleep in his barn for the night if we would be careful not to smoke cigarettes anywhere near the barn. With our friends' help, we did a little outside campfire cooking and then all bedded down upstairs in the barn where plenty of good, clean hay was available for a bed.

The next day stands out in my memory even today—just as clear as if it just happened. It was a beautiful sunny day, and we all knew that work for everyone was just a few miles away. We weren't sure where the work was, so we just piled into the car and started driving. Our goal was to pick out a farm that was well kept with plenty of fruit trees.

After a few miles we selected a farm that appeared to have just what we were looking for. The home itself was large and absolutely beautiful with a huge red barn and other machine sheds that made us feel that this farmer would surely need help.

We pulled over to the side of the road in front of one farm and Dad went up to the house and knocked on the door and an elderly man answered. In just a few seconds, the farmer came out to look us over to make sure we had enough people old enough to do the work that needed to be done. Once he saw the three older boys, his eyes lit up with the realization that good cheap labor had arrived.

1937 – 1945

This was our introduction to Nelson Feathers, Sr. He told us that he owned the land, but his son, Nelson, Jr. ran the place and would make the final decision. He sent someone to get his son. And when his son arrived, he saw the potential fruit pickers and a deal was made. We had a job for everyone and I had not ever seen that much joy in Mom and Dad's faces.

Mr. Feathers told us that the only place he had for us to live was in a machine shed that he pointed to up on the top of a hill about one hundred yards away. He said it just needed cleaning, but he thought it would be suitable.

We all went up to the hill to the shed, that later became known as the shed house, and rolled back the huge sliding door that would open up wide enough to let a tractor drive through.

The place didn't look all that bad, and the potential for a fairly nice place to live during the summer looked pretty good. A handrail straight-up step to the loft gave us a way to get to the hay loft. The big old loft looked great to me because the floor was solid and the gate style door at one end was well built.

We spent all day washing and cleaning the shed with disinfectant. Dad went to the store and bought some lunch meat and pork and beans for supper and milk, cereal, and sweet rolls for breakfast the next morning.

The next day Mr. Feathers helped us put in a cookstove and a couple of beds for Mom, Dad, and my sister. We took some large sheets and walled off the downstairs into a kitchen and two bedrooms that provided some semblance of semi-privacy. The six of us boys got straw ticks and filled them with straw and had more room than we had ever had in our lives in our upstairs loft.

Picking fruit is purely an incentive program. The more you pick, the more you get paid. My mom, dad, sister, and the three older brothers would go pick cherries while Max, Brent, and I stayed home and kept the house.

The money started coming in and things really began to look good. After the cherries came the red and black raspberries. I was allowed (made) to go work and put in ten hours a day—just like everyone else. It took two people to a row to pick. I was paired with Dad, and he kept me busy. To break the monotony, he would let me have a few drags off his cigarette when Mama wasn't around. I developed the smoking habit that I kept until 1968.

After strawberries, the peaches came in, and even though I was too young to climb the ladder and pick, I did go into the orchard with fresh water and help move the ladder and the fruit for my family. My mother and sister worked in the sorting and packing shed at an hourly rate and our savings were beginning to accumulate. We were really having a great time and with money and good food to eat, everything began to look good.

There were a number of "Arkies," as we were called in the area, and we got to know them from meeting at the country store just down the road at a place called Hinchman, Michigan. Since the locals didn't really want to socialize with us "Arkies," we stuck together as a different stratum of society. They were not unkind to us; it was simply that we were different, and they weren't sure about us.

We worked six days a week and sometimes on Sunday if the fruit was ripe and had to be picked. There was a saying that we would work from "can" to "can't" while the getting was good. There would be plenty of time to rest when winter came.

It wasn't all work, and we began to find out where we could go for the least amount of money. Every Wednesday there was a "free" outdoor movie shown in the downtown park in Baroda, Michigan. We started going to that every week. Shortly after, we started going to Bridgman every Friday night where there was "free" outdoor championship wrestling. The local merchants sponsored these activities so that the hundreds of "Arkies" would come in and spend their money. It must have been successful because these programs were well supported each week. We got to meet a lot of young boys our age and sometimes we would all meet and take our slingshots and go bird hunting.

There were a number of great places to go swimming every time we could get away long enough to go. There was a fine local lake just a couple of miles away called "Singer Lake" and it was spring-fed. This meant the water was fresh and very cold, even during the hottest days of summer. The lake was very deep, and we enjoyed this often.

Lake Michigan was only about ten miles away, and an amusement park called "Silver Beach" was right on Lake Michigan and was a great place to go and spend the day. There were all kinds of amusement park rides on the grounds, and we would swim in Lake Michigan and then ride the rides, and by late afternoon we would all be dead tired.

Indian Lake was another place we visited because it had a huge slide into the water and a park where we could put our food out and have a picnic. We really enjoyed living in this part of the country, and I know our family was happier than we had ever been in our lives.

When the peaches got ripe, everyone was working except Max, Brent, and me. My mother and sister worked in the peach shed sorting and packing the peaches in bushel baskets. Brent would stay in the shed with Mom, and Max and I were left to run around and just have fun. We would go swimming at Singer Lake or take our slingshots and go out in the woods and shoot at targets.

In September, the weather began to get pretty cold, and we started thinking about going back to Arkansas for the winter. We all knew that we could go home and pick cotton until mid-November, and then get by until spring when we could return to the fruit farm in Michigan.

Just after Labor Day, we began to pack up for the trip home. This time we had two cars to take back to Arkansas. Mr. Nelson agreed to hold our place for the following spring and to let us leave any personal belongings we wished in the shed on his farm.

We returned to Arkansas and rented a small home and just kind of picked up where we left off.

As soon as we got back to Leachville, Max, Brent, and I enrolled in school. Tom, Harlan, Vane, and Evelyn had already dropped out of school with only limited educations. None of the three boys had ever gone to high school, and Evelyn dropped out in tenth grade. We were behind the other kids in school, and it was tough trying to catch up, but we had no choice but to try.

In the spring of 1938, we left for Michigan in April and left school to make the trip back north. We knew that if we got back to Michigan early enough, we could pick strawberries by the crate and make "good money."

By now, we were very experienced at this kind of moving, and we were going back to familiar territory. But the attitude of everyone was much different this time. We were more aware and more confident than we had been a year earlier. We had grown and felt that any situation that developed could be coped with by our family successfully.

Our second year in Michigan went much better for other social reasons, too. Max and I enrolled in a local one-room school in Hinchman, and this opened up the door to meeting some of the farm children from the area. While they were not prone to accept migrant worker children as their equals, the additional contact did help the situation some. School was tough for us, and I dreaded going every day. We were behind in mathematics, and catching up was nearly impossible. Clearly, Max and I were maturing at a rapid rate, and tour-developed experiences gave us a confidence level unique for our age level.

When the 1938 fruit season ended in late September, we headed south and home again. On the way down, we stopped at Dad's brother's farm in Sikeston, Missouri near the wide spot in the road called McMullin. His name was Will Dye and he was a sharecropper in the area. "Uncle Bill," as he was affectionally called by everyone in the area, was really an outstanding person and stands out clearly in my mind even today. Uncle Bill could not read or write at all even though he had a keen mind and a memory that was near-total recall. Even though he could not write anything down, it was said that he could judge a hog's weight with almost total accuracy and estimate its worth to the penny. I can recall Uncle Bill taking his signature out of his billfold and copying his signature so he could sign his checks. Uncle Bill was ten years older than Dad, and they had never been close since they were separated most of their lives.

Anyway, we stopped to see Uncle Bill and Aunt Lou, on the way home. While we were there visiting, Dad heard of a nice farm six miles north that was looking for a sharecropping family. We went up and looked it over and it looked pretty good to us, so Dad made a deal with the landlord and we moved in.

This farm was located about three miles west of Highway 61 on Baseline Road; this road is just south of Morley, Missouri and the farm was in the Morley School District.

Morley, Missouri was then, and still is, a small town in the foothills of the Ozarks and the land flattens out at Morley and stays flat all of the way south through Arkansas and most of Mississippi.

I don't think Dad knew it at the time, but the farm we had agreed to sharecrop was made up of a lot of sand and turned out to be so poor that you couldn't raise an umbrella on it. The land down around McMullen just few miles south was much better farmland. However, we were real pleased to have a place to farm again, and Dad seemed especially pleased and proud to have a decent-looking house to move his family into. That happiness was short-lived because our landowner boss, E.P. Coleman, was not a man that believed sharecroppers were anything better than white trash.

His mannerisms and treatment of Dad from the very beginning was harsh and demeaning, seemingly designed to crush the spirit. Since neither Dad nor Mom were the kind to knuckle under, that relationship never had a chance for development or survival.

The school bus came right to the front of the house, so I was enrolled in the sixth grade at Morley Consolidated School. This was a fine experience because I had two of the best teachers I have ever met. Mrs. Ruth Lee and Mrs. Lett probably are remembered by every student they had pass through their classrooms. Unfortunately for me, I only attended Morley for one year because we moved again before I started the seventh grade.

Life on the sharecropper's place on baseline road was pretty rough. We didn't have any money and the land was so poor that we knew we would be moving on at the first opportunity. The small town of Oran was just a few miles north us us and it had a popular "picture show house" that we could walk the four miles each Saturday and pay a dime to attend. The theatre was upstairs over a furniture store and every Saturday we would fill up the stairs with people waiting for the one o'clock opening of the ticket window.

My first encounter with equal opportunity happened one Saturday when a young man and a "swamp angel" in front of me approached the window. The young man said "gimme one ticket" and the girl said, "Why Vestal, ain't you gonna buy me my ticket?"

And the young man replied, "I ain't buying you nary ticket. Shoot far, you can pick as much as I can." All of us waiting in line got a kick out of that.

When the spring of 1938 rolled around, the urge to go back to Michigan to pick fruit began to hit all of us. The hardships of Michigan was preferable to living on a poor, non-productive farm in S.E. Missouri. The Dortch family in Leachville, Arkansas notified us that they would be coming through in a one and one-half ton truck and would have room to pick us up to ride in the rear if we wanted to go back up north with them. We did, so we loaded up and got our old place in the tool shed on the hill at the Feathers farm just outside of Hinchman, Michigan.

We stayed in Michigan, as always, until cold weather came and then headed south to help pick cotton and go to school. We found an old house just almost two miles from McMullan (six miles north of Sickeston) and I started school in Blodgett, a small town about fifteen miles from home. Max and I had to walk to the main Highway 61 to catch the bus, and this was rough during cold weather. I can remember trying tow sacks (burlap bags) around my shoes when snow was on the ground because my tennis shoes would get wet, and the cold would be unbearable.

The old house or shack that we lived in should have been condemned, but it was the best we could do. I was tickled to see spring come so we could head back to Michigan.

I don't know what happened between us and the Feathers family, but they wouldn't give us our place, so we found a farm to work on a couple of miles from there and had plenty of work.

The cement block shed we moved into was so small that us boys slept in the barn at night and ate our meals in the house. It would have been pretty rough if we had known better, but we didn't.

This was to be our last trip to Michigan until the spring of 1944, because when we went back in the fall of 1944 to southeast Missouri, we landed a sharecropper's place on the McMullen Estate just off of Highway 61 six miles north of Sikeston at the wide place in the road of McMullen, which boasted a large general store, a cotton gin, and a mechanics garage.

There were a lot of good things about this stroke of good fortune.

The main thing was the fine old two-story house that had more rooms than we had ever had before. Brent, Max, and I shared one room and Vane, Harlan, and Tom shared a room and Sis had a room all to herself. The next three years were the happiest of my life up until that time. Even though we were sharecroppers, the McMullen Estate allowed us to raise hogs and chickens and grow our own vegetables for canning. The place had a huge barn for the mules and feed and grain. It had another barn for the cows and hogs, plus a smokehouse and chicken house, and a single room shack for housing the black people that would help us with picking the cotton in the fall.

I think the point in painting a picture of the farm buildings is to illustrate that even though we were sharecroppers, I felt like we were finally in a situation where we fitted into the highest level of the very poor. It put us in a situation where we felt that none could look down on us.

Our contract was to grow cotton on 120 acres of land for the plantation called McMullen Estate. We had two teams of mules for Dad and Harlan while the rest of us chopped the cotton to keep the weeds out. It was good, rich soil, and the yield usually ran a bale to one and one-half bales to the acre. It was a great time because all six boys, Sis, Mom, and Dad had a closeness that made family life a lot of fun. I started in the seventh grade at Blodgett High School and stayed there until I graduated. The school was twelve miles away and the school bus was a lot of fun, even though we left early and got home late.

In 1941, a huge truck stop and café was built at McMullen that was called "Grant City Truck Stop and Café." This was an excellent restaurant, and the truckers made this one of their favorite stops. The Bar-B-Que sandwich was a specialty and the townspeople from Sikeston would drive the six miles out to Grant City to eat the Bar-B-Que. I was hired as a curb hop at ten cents per hour and would chop cotton and work on the farm until noon on Saturdays and then work from noon until midnight and Sundays from 11 a.m. until 11 p.m. and loved it. My sister Evelyn was there as a waitress. I was so proud of her because she was so pretty, smart, and could handle her own with a bunch of truckers looking for a hustle.

The Impact of Pearl Harbor

The major turning point in this part of our life occurred in 1941 on December 7, when the Japanese attacked Pearl Harbor and America entered World War II. Harlan and Vane left to go to St. Louis because war production plants were opening, and good jobs were rapidly becoming available. Sis had got a job in town and Tom was restless to get out on his own. It became apparent that the boss man on the plantation didn't like losing all that cheap farm labor.

This was a sad time because Max, Brent, and I really enjoyed going with Mom and Dad every Saturday night to a honky-tonk called Kluge Hall and watching Harlen, Vane, and Tom cut a rug dancing to the jukebox filled with the best country music of the time.

Every Saturday night, you could almost be assured of seeing two or three good fights after the beer got most of the men tanked up. The owner didn't mind the fights as long as they went outside. I saw a few good fights where knives were used and saw one man literally have his stomach ripped open one night. I never did find out if he lived or died.

I remember that Vane was a good fighter with a pretty mean temper and most of the locals gave him plenty of room when he was around. I always thought that the rest of us were kind of scared of him when he got into a bad mood. I know I was, and was more than a little awed by his ability to handle himself. On the other hand, he never seemed to be close to anyone and didn't develop any close friends that I can remember.

In the fall of 1942, we were asked to move, and Dad found another sharecrop farm up at Brook's Junction about four miles north of Grant City. The house was pretty scary, and the land value was even worse. This took out of the Blodgett School District by about one and one-half miles and meant we would have to enroll in Morley again. This was a disaster from the standpoint of how Max and I felt because we wanted to stay enrolled at Blodgett High School. So we walked three miles a day to catch the Blodgett School bus.

The summer of 1943 was a difficult time because Tom and Vane were in the Army and Harlan had a job in St. Louis. Harlan and Vane and Tom had all married. Evelyn was working for the J.C. Penney Company in Sikeston. After we got the crops laid by, I went into Sikeston and got a job at the Army Air Corp Training Base as a busboy and washed dishes, pots, and pans all summer. This was a job that beat the stew out of working on the farm, and the good food that we were allowed to eat was an extra bonus.

When school started in September, I quit the busboy job and went into the eleventh grade at Blodgett High School. This was my best year in school. Since I was a little over six feet tall and my basketball skills had improved enough, I made the team as a forward. Basketball was the big thing in rural areas and was about the only team sport that received spectator support. We played basketball year-round and the competition between us and Morley, Benton, Vanuser, Oran, and Dillstadt was often heated.

My junior year had a pretty fair team, and we knew we would be real good my senior year because we had another junior class player named Monroe Wheeler that was six foot, four inches tall, and he was a good player. His younger brother, a sophomore, Don Wheeler was already the best player on the team, and we had another sophomore named David Seitz that couple play point guard as well as anyone in the county. I was not a good outside shooter but could play inside well enough to make a contribution and could get the ball to Monroe, who was tall enough to jump over anyone we played.

For the record, I never saw anyone in high school that could jump high enough to dunk the ball.

In the summer of 1944, Mom, Dad, Max, Brent, and I headed back to Michigan and got a job on the Marske farm. This was a fine old German family that had a large peach and apple farm.

In July of that year, Max and I were permitted to go into Berrain Springs and get a job at a large defense plant. We worked there until it was time to go back to Missouri and go to school. I had turned eighteen years of age on July 21, 1944, and registered for the draft. I never dreamed that I would be drafted and did not file for a deferment. I was stunned when I got my draft notice and had to report to Jefferson City for the Army on November 12, 1944. Whatever might have been for our basketball team had to give way while I served my country in the war effort.

The day I was drafted was a beautiful day and I had orders to catch the Greyhound bus in Benton, Missouri. Dad and I pulled bales that morning and I got my last bath in that old Number 2 bathtub before he took me up to the Courthouse in Benton. None of this bothered me much because, I suppose, we had moved so much that a transient situation with a lot of unknowns was not a new experience for me.

We were only at Jefferson Barracks for two days before being sent to Camp Hood, Texas for our seventeen weeks of basic infantry training. We had finished receiving a medical examination, got all of our uniforms and basic instructions on how to pack up on the troop train headed for Texas, and seventeen weeks of tough training.

We were a pretty sorry-looking group because none of the uniforms fit except the shoes. It was obvious some of us were expected to gain weight while others were expected to lose a few pounds. When you looked around at your fellow soldiers your first thought was "Oh boy, I hope I don't have to go into battle with this bunch!"

The seventeen weeks of training would change all of that just as it was designed to do.

I was probably one of the few people that enjoyed infantry basic training. I did not have a problem with getting up at five o'clock in the morning and hiking all day, it never fazed me. The field problems were fun, and the only problem I had learning was how to take a rifle apart and put it back together. I never got the hang of that in spite of doing it over and over and over again. However, I did well enough on everything else that our Company Commander offered me a chance at going to Officer Candidate School. When he said that all I would have to do was pass an examination aimed at the two years of college-level, I declined the opportunity. I knew that my academics were too inferior for that kind of test. I was, however, selected to attend the Advanced Specialized Training Program at Fort Knox, Kentucky.

While I was at Fort Knox, the war ended along with the need for all special training. I became a replacement for the rotation plan so that the men in Europe could come home.

I finally landed at Le Havre, France and was put on a box car headed for Germany.

We went through France into Germany where I was eventually stationed at Sonthofen in Bavaria.

The train trip across France, Belgium, into Germany for most of the men I was put with was very hard for them. The boxcars were of the small generation box cars called 408s. This denomination came from WWI intruding to denote you would haul 40 men and 8 horses in each boxcar.

Since horses were no longer used in the military, we loaded the box cars down with all the soldiers and duffel bags we could pack into the car. They gave us rations of C and K for the trip. The "K-Ration" contained food, candy, and cigarettes, while the "C-Ration" was filled with food that had to be heated. We had a stove in the boxcar for heating our C-Rations that not was a problem. Some of us would jump off of the train when it slowed down at a junction and run alongside for exercise. It was a boring two days, and I was glad when we arrived in Kempton, Germany to be loaded onto 6 X6 trucks to be carried to Sonthofen, Germany for my European tour of duty.

Traveling across France gave me an opportunity to see the devastation the war had caused. The war had just ended in May and we were arriving to relieve all the combat teams of people anxious to go home. My brother Vane had been killed in January 1945 and traveling through the area close to where he had been killed gave me a strange feeling. And Brother Tom was still "somewhere in Germany" but I had no way of even hoping to find him.

We did not get to really meet with the French people traveling through in our boxcar. However, it was obvious that they had not gotten themselves organized to clean up the devastation caused by the shelling of their area by competing German and American Armies. You did have a strong feeling of comradeship for these people that had suffered so long under a German occupation that was extremely harsh and even cruel at times.

When we arrived in Germany it was obvious that the train, we came in on would be used to take a bunch of combat troops back to LeHavire, France to fill up the ship we came over on.

These soldiers were fired up and ready to come home and the difference in their appearance and that of us Greenhorns were vividly obvious.

They still carried their sidearms and M-1 rifles with live ammunition, and there was enough free wine, beer, and champagne available to keep a party going for them around the clock. We were told to stay quiet, stay still, and stay out of the way.

I was scared enough to know I did not want to tangle with a combat veteran that wouldn't hold his liquor and had a war hangover anger of some kind.

Enough of this remembrance of the troops from LeHavre to Kempton, Germany.

Sonthofen, Germany is located in Bavaria and its key major city is Munich. Bavaria is an extremely beautiful area and is steeped in the history of Nazi Germany. I won't dwell on that because history books cover this thoroughly.

I will spend some writing time explaining my perception of the German people that might shed a small view of what they are, or may be, and why they are able to do what they do. It is important to keep in mind that all of my military training was directed toward giving me a perception as to why I should hate the Germans, and the killing of my brother simply added to that feeling of hate. And I feel some disappointment that I could never "get even" for my brother's death. I think every soldier would have felt that way to some degree.

Sonthofen is high up in the Alps and the scenery in that area is absolutely breathtaking. Hitler accepted Sonthofen as the place to build a youth training center for 12-to-14-year-old boys that would be the leadership of the future 1,000 year Reich. When you enter the university you pass through an arch into a large quadrangle surrounded by a three-story dormitory for the students and absolutely beautiful administrative, classroom, mess hall, and gymnasium facilities. The production of leaders for the military from these "Hitler Jugend" training facilities explains why the German Army was without question the best trained in the world.

I was assigned to the 3rd Army in Kempton and our battalion was sent to Sonthofen with the goal of getting the

"Hitler Youth Center" prepared to convert to the "School of Geopolitical Science" to train American officers on how to convert Germany into a future democracy. The enlisted men occupied the student dormitory with two men to a room. Each floor had enough "putzen frau" (cleaning women) to keep rooms and facilities spotlessly clean. The Putzen Frau thought nothing about opening a shower door while you were bathing to see if you had enough soap. They always would walk into the bathroom at any time and thought nothing about it. I never got used to that.

After a few days, I needed some laundry done and asked my sergeant where the laundry was located. He said, "Corporal Dye, you go out to the main gate around dark tonight and pick out one of the German women out there begging for work. They will do a great job for a package of cigarettes and a bar of soap. And don't you dare to do more than that."

I went out to the main gate and picked out a young woman about twenty-four years old and she became my wash lady the whole time I was there. After a few weeks of knowing her, I learned that her husband had been killed in the war leaving her with two little boys, six and four years of age. One day, I went to the PX and bought soap, Prince Albert smoking tobacco, a lot of candy, and a few cans of food and went to her house to give her and her kids a gift. She became very upset and refused the gift because she wanted her kids to learn that you "must work" for everything you get. I left and later got her to do some work on my uniforms and gave her the "gift" in payment. Her attitude, I learned, was not unusual.

The German people were defeated, but they maintained a very high degree of pride in themselves, their country, and their leaders. They lost, but they were not beaten.

That German spirit manifested itself in many ways. In all of the months that we all lived in the dormitory, I never heard of a simple case of anything being stolen from our rooms. Everywhere I went, I saw Germans cleaning up bricks from buildings destroyed by artillery shells during the war. Those bricks were being stacked up for future use, but there was not any apparent buyer or plans for immediate use. In my conversations with many workmen, I would ask, "Why are you doing this?" They would look at me as if I had asked a stupid question and simply say, "It must be done."

We had access to vehicles, mostly WWII Jeeps that were abandoned during the war. We would ride all around Bavaria visiting castles, old breweries, and resort areas that were still active. Since there was no government except the U.S. Army, everything we saw and wanted we simply took it. We were permitted to have and carry weapons but never had to use them. The Germans had the attitude of "We lost the war. You won it so let us get on with life." As a result, I think we began to really respect the people because they showed a class of grace that we did not expect. I'll never forget the one time when three of us jumped in a Jeep and drove to Berchtesgaden to see Hitler's retreat. We just walked into that beautiful hotel and told the people in charge to clear out three of their best rooms. We just spent one night there, but the food and hospitality were great. We did not even think of paying for anything, nor did the Germans expect us to. They thanked us for not going nuts and tearing up the place. It was obvious that this had happened before, and the Germans needed to protect the beautiful old hotel.

There was a favorite place we went to often during the summer months. It was a small inn on the bank of a lake in a small town near Sonthofen. The inn was under the supervision of the U.S. Army and was run by a competent German staff. A fine motorboat was available and three of us would go there often.

Our unit began the training of Army officers that would be assigned at the state, county, and local levels to literally run a country until a Democratic form of Government could be installed. My job was to perform "grunt" duties for the officers operating the Department of Geopolitics and the training for personnel.

Bobby Dye's Perspective of His Dad

My dad, Spence Dye, took advantage of the G.I. Bill by using it to attend college at Murray State University in Murray, Kentucky, where he was president of both his class and fraternity. He was the first member of his family to graduate from college.

The majority of his career was spent at Southern Bell Telephone and Telegraph Company, where he met a woman—a "drop-dead gorgeous woman" whom he married—Billie Lee Gliessner. They were married in August of 1954 and went on to have three children—Jim, LeAnn, and Bobby—who gave them numerous grandchildren and great-grandchildren.

After the breakup of the Bell system in 1982, he left to run the Mississippi Retail Association.

Later, he started his own company, Spence Dye Consulting, LLC, where he was an independent lobbyist in Mississippi and Washington, D.C. He was respected on both sides of the aisle. He would tell people, "You can call me a Liberal Republican or a Conservative Democrat!"

He did not care which. He was instead, a seeker of unity and peace and knew instinctively how to reach all walks of life – the rich and the poor.

His pastimes were spent helping people—particularly in golf. He became a member of the Country Club of Jackson,

Mississippi. He developed a close relationship with his son, Bobby.

"We were more like brothers than father and son," Spence Dye often said.

"We were friends—but I always treated him with respect," I would say about my dad "He was fair and loving towards us. There were a lot of things that he passed on to me from a working standpoint that taught me how to work with people and to be appreciative."

Spence Dye became a member of the Country Club of Jackson, Mississippi, where one of his greatest accomplishments was 11 holes-in-one.

He wanted people to succeed and did what he could to help.

On his deathbed, Spence Dye praised the healthcare workers who took care of him.

It was a typical response for a man whose roots began with next to nothing—and common for a boy whose mother would tell him while growing up, to remember where they came from.

He never forgot—he just added to the heritage.

Likewise, he would tell his children and grandchildren the same.

Dad was a man led by his faith. He wasn't a man to quote scripture, but he was a man that lived it. He was at peace with his afterlife. He had faith in his life and accepted Christ. He wasn't a Bible-thumper, but he lived his life by example and saw the good in others, even those who didn't show it very well.

Consequently, I always open the Dye Resource Management meetings on Monday mornings with a prayer to help people—either motivating, encouraging, or financially helping whoever is in need.

Spence Dye died on July 27, 2018.

In his last hours of life, as he lay in his hospital bed, Spence Dye motioned me to step close. I put my head close to his, and he placed his hand on my chest. He gently took my hand and placed it upon his own chest.

He whispered, "One heart."

It is one heart and three generations that continues the legacy today.

CHAPTER 2

A Woman of Her Word

From Bobby Dye's perspective:

Billie Lee Gliessner Dye—Spence Dye's wife of sixty-four years—is the personality opposite of her husband.

He was gregarious.

She kept more to herself, but was the glue that always brought the Dye family together.

She grew up in a middle-class family during the Great Depression. Her father, Carl Gliessner, worked for the Hillerich and Bradsby Co.—the company that made Louisville Slugger bats and PowerBilt golf clubs in Louisville, Kentucky. He worked in the pro golf division.

Once she married Spence Dye, she worked to bring order into her growing family, watching pennies, and teaching her children and grandchildren the value of working toward their dreams.

She was a homemaker all her life—for her kids and grandkids.

Every morning, she made her children a big breakfast—toast, bacon, and eggs—and packed paper bag lunches filled with peanut butter and jelly sandwiches, chips, and fruit. She would bring me milkshakes as I did my homework.

Every night, there was a full meal on the table.

She had a more affluent childhood than my dad. They were not rich by any means, but they were more middle class.

So, when we were growing up, Dad would be at work, and we would answer to her. If we did something wrong, we had to wait until Dad came home—which meant he was going to lay down the law. But she was the one who always held me accountable. When I was struggling to work on my writing skills, doing cursive writing, she had me do the alphabet and get every letter exactly right.

It had to be done right. No exceptions.

When I was done, I could then go outside and play basketball, or just get outside and play.

She was the one who took care of us. She was a mama bear. She was protective of us, even when we were wrong. She would always defend us. She was very protective of her children and grandchildren.

She was always Mom. We could count on her.

She was the type that, whenever we were eating dinner, if the food ran out, Mom would always act like she was not hungry and would not finish any until the kids had finished eating.

It would drive me nuts because I would slow down eating because I didn't want my mom to be hungry.

She was a workhorse when it came to her children. She was a disciplinarian and would encourage you to go out and play with the guys who were bigger and tougher. She would not allow me to back down. I was always expected to do my best, no less, and then be happy with the result.

Growing up, she would encourage us. She would always tell us to do our best. That's all she expected, and she was happy with that. She would say, "Only your best is good enough." There might be other little boys who could do something better, and she'd say that's fine. But she'd encourage me to get out there and do my best, anyhow. If you'd get discouraged, she'd be the encourager and encourage you to work harder. She would push us on to get better.

Sometimes, I wonder where I got my mindset or discipline and structure—I think I got a combination of her German heritage and my dad. It's a good blend.

She did everything to keep the family going while Dad was having to go to work every day. He would come home and work in his chair until he fell asleep.

The spotlight was always on him, but she was and is the glue who makes the whole family come together.

She is the one who started our annual beach trips. We call it Christmas in July, when the whole family comes together for several days on an Alabama beach at either Gulf Shores, or Orange Beach. It's an annual trip that was started in the early 1980s. It was family time—a time the family still gets together and has grown as our family has grown.

What I Learned Growing Up

Until her death, Mom still balanced her checkbook down to the penny. She would literally go to the bank if it was a penny off. Mom and Dad made a great combination because Mom saved money and Dad was always making money to give away. She paid the bills, and she did the taxes. She was the one who kind of did everything from the standpoint of managing the house.

When I was eight years old, she taught me to manage money and use it wisely.

I wanted a bike and had saved a little money. But it was springtime and I just wanted to be outdoors. I didn't have all the money for the bike—some of it, but not all of it. I had to borrow money from my mom to buy it.

I wrote her a promissory note and paid her back with my allowance.

It was a contract, I had to sign as a responsibility—I was only eight years old!

I still have that note in a file. As I work with clients today, I'm able to understand and see both sides of how my mom and dad operated, or, at least, their perspectives on how they viewed money. When you are working with a client, you read them carefully.

Some people are like my mom, very tight with their money. Some are like my dad. You read them not only for body language, but you learn to understand when they are anxious about what you are saying.

I think it is dangerous for an advisor to be one-sided in their opinion on money. My mom taught me to be careful and disciplined about protecting money, but many people don't have that same discipline with their savings.

She has always lived by example—caring, loving, and protecting the family. She knew who wanted things for Christmas, how we would do decorations, and every other small detail. She could be pretty strict, and would not hesitate to tell us when we couldn't afford something, but she took such good care of us. Her love for us was unmatched, and I can never fully pay her back for what she's done for us.

Dad was my buddy, but Mom is Mom. She held us to a certain standard. When I graduated from high school, my dad's parents sent me a $1 bill. It was a big deal. It's still in my safe deposit box. I keep it as a reminder.

My parents sacrificed to send me to a private school when I was in high school. When all my friends went to Europe and were getting nice cars after graduation, I got that $1 bill and it meant more to me than anything because I knew where it was coming from, and I knew how hard they worked to earn that dollar.

And that stuck with me.

You don't forget where you come from.

The End of an Era

After Dad's death, Mom struggled with Lewy Body Dementia, a progressive decline of mental and physical abilities.

My mother died Nov. 2, 2021.

She really surprised me before she died in that she was a lot stronger than I realized. At my daughter Laura's wedding, my mother looked absolutely stunning. But at the end of the wedding, she raised up her hands and said, "That's it, I'm done."

And, at nearly eighty-eight years old, she meant she was done with life.

My daughter's wedding was Oct. 16, 2021.

It was one of those weddings you save up twenty years for—it was a full blown-out affair. The reception was in our backyard and there was a nice, beautiful sunset. We had a band playing music until 10 o'clock.

What made it all worth it was that my mother was there—something she vowed she would live for.

The best part for me was at the wedding in the church when they announced the couple. My daughter came down the stairs—left her new husband—and went to my mother and gave her a kiss on the cheek. She thanked her for "being there." They were very close. Then, Laura went back to her husband, and they took off.

At that moment, there wasn't a dry eye in the church.

Everybody started crying at once.

My mother just froze and put her hands to her face and started crying, she was so happy.

It was at that moment that any cost of the wedding was no longer a concern, and what my mother received from my daughter was far greater than anything in this world to her.

I told my wife afterward that I thought it was the best wedding I'd ever been to.

About four or five days after the wedding, my mom fell.

We didn't think it was anything major. There was no head trauma or anything like that. She had no complaints and we got her back up into bed.

But about three or four days after that, her neck hurt really bad. We got her into the ambulance and to the hospital. The X-Ray showed she had fractured her neck in three places. The doctor said if she had moved a certain way, she would have been a quadriplegic.

He explained that the ligaments that held her neck up eventually got tired, and that's when the pain started. She did not want to go to the hospital and was very combative about it, which only made it worse.

My mom had made up her mind to go home. In the emergency room, she looked at me and smiled.

She said, "You really love your mother, don't you?"

I took my mask off and said, "Yes, Mom, I really do."

Later on, when we got her to her room, she was really struggling. She had on a neck brace and was medicated. It was just awful because I didn't want her to struggle.

She tried to say something, and I put my ear down next to her mouth and she said, "I love you."

My sister heard it.

I said, "Mom, I heard you, I heard you!"

It was the best gift.

It was also ... the last thing she said to me.

It was to tell me she loved me. I knew she did. It wasn't like I needed to hear her affirmation.

And she knew I loved her.

But I never knew until then what a goal-setter she was. She had certain goals, and she set her life on this one.

There is a saying that you can't cry over answered prayers.

And this was one of those prayers.

After she died, I found her Bible, and inside was the original unfinished copy of this chapter I wrote about her.

She passed away only 17 days after the wedding. She, as always, kept her word to be there. She was ready to go, and she did that too. She was a strong woman and the best mom ever.

I miss her every day.

Nobody loves you like your mother, nobody!

I miss her every day—but what I miss most is her love for me.

A mother's love.

CHAPTER 3

Chasing Your Vision Includes Teamwork

In high school and college, I played center on the football team, the innermost position on the offensive line. We are the ones who snap the ball to the quarterback at the start of each play.

But there is more to it than that. There is a certain honor and code to being a center. The role of the center is to gather the offensive team into a huddle.

When a play is over, the center goes back 10 yards from the line of scrimmage, raises his arms and yells "Huddle up!"

The center brings everybody together. The quarterback then walks into the huddle and calls the play.

As a center, I'd break the huddle and we'd go to the line. I'd call the colors, the plays, and the blocking schemes. The center is the quarterback of the offensive line.

Years later, I use this experience to bring everyone together to organize a strategy for my business.

Hall of fame coach Vince Lombardi said that for a team to be successful, they must work in a coordinated efficiency. They need to be coordinated, they need to be efficient, and they need to work together.

That's the mindset of an offensive lineman. Our assignment is to do all the hard work, and then let somebody else have all the glory.

We could be the driving force behind moving the ball ninety-nine yards downfield, then let someone else score the touchdown. Others may get the recognition and awards, but offensive linemen take pride knowing they couldn't have done it without us.

Everyone in the huddle has a different job to do. No one person can do the job of every player on the team. Everyone has their own skillset. Linemen block. Wide receivers catch the ball. Running backs run—and so on.

In our office, it's the same way. It's important to know what your particular skillset is. It is also important to know what your weaknesses are. You hire people who have strengths that are your weaknesses.

This makes for a team of strengths—with no weak links.

Our office manager is our central hub. She coordinates everything. Mandy Harkins is the hardest worker I've ever been associated with in my career. She has high expectations of herself and expects the same from those in the office. She has a college degree and is a success story. Our clients love her, and she makes herself available to them six days a week.

Every team needs a person who will push to get better. She also keeps it fun too. Her work ethic in running the office allows me to focus on my skillset of helping people to achieve their financial goals.

I have always been somewhat of a loner. I had to do things my way. I've learned over several years what worked and what didn't. It took me a couple of years to trust her to run my office. I was reluctant to let go. Once I did, I knew I could trust her, and it was the best decision I made. The office was being managed more efficiently and I was allowed to focus on the skills I was good at doing and productivity skyrocketed.

Her strengths were my weaknesses, and my strengths were her weaknesses. It was great teamwork. Not only are we producing, but work is enjoyable. Our clients benefit the most. It's all part of teamwork and the coordinated efficiency that Lombardi talked about. Trust is required for a team to be successful.

Trusting each teammate to do their job as you do yours: one missed assignment and the team fails. It all starts in the huddle.

Seeing the Vision

When it comes to having goals, you first must have a vision. Sometimes the two can be confused for each other.

I believe you must have a vision to know where you want to go or what you are trying to achieve. You must feel led or inspired.

Once you establish your vision, then you can visualize it into existence. You can start setting up goals—how to achieve them in short-term, intermediate, long-term, and ultimate goals.

- Short-term goals are achieved day to day or week to week.
- Intermediate might be six months to a year.
- And long-term can be achieved in ten years or more.
- What's your ultimate goal? It's your final, ultimate objective.

Your vision is what drives you in the morning when you wake up. The goal is what drives it day by day.

Business is different because there can be finite goals. They may be forty and sixty years in the making, but doable.

I set a high standard for myself. I want to go as far in life from where I started as my dad did in his lifetime. Where my dad came from and what he did was extraordinary.

For me to achieve that from where I started would be extra extraordinary, because I had a huge advantage. I started out way ahead compared to where my father started. He didn't have anything—so that drove him to have something.

My disadvantage is that I did have something, which can make it harder to have that same drive. The example set by my father motivates me to do my best every single day. This is required of me if I ever stand a chance to match him.

On Setting Goals

Everything I do, and that I have stressed with my children while they were growing up, is about having a vision.

Where do you want to go? Goals should be obtained day-by-day, minute-to-minute, not overnight.

The achievers break it down into smaller pieces. Like eating an elephant—you can only do it one bite at a time.

Achieving a goal requires an unusual amount of discipline and sacrifice to do the things you *need* to do rather than what you sometimes may *want* to do. Growing up, it might have meant not going out with my friends at night. It was about doing what I had to get done so I could enjoy achieving the goal.

It is a single-mindedness that you sometimes wake up thinking about after you go to sleep at night. It's all-encompassing.

You ask yourself, "Have I done everything I could today to be successful. Do I feel good about the day?"

Even as a boy, I remember sitting and thinking about the different types of people—analyzing why they did things, and why they acted a certain way. I watched people closely. I remember thinking I could figure people out—watch their mannerisms and body language, and what they would say—

and I could figure out if they were a good person or not. Did they have ulterior motives? Did they have a kind heart?

I learned early on that I could read people—and had a gift of intuition.

But I also had an ability to work hard and self-discipline.

I purposely did things the hard way. My thought was if I did things the hard way, it would make me stronger—so I would look at ways to challenge myself mentally and physically.

When I was in high school, I had a focus. I had a vision or dream of what I wanted to achieve by my senior year in football.

I would do things that nobody else knew I was doing. Some nights—on Fridays or Saturdays—I would sneak out to the school, climb the fence, and go into the weight room at 11 p.m. to work out. To me, I was getting ahead. While others might be out partying or doing stuff, I was getting ahead.

I'd also go run or jog. As a lineman, running was not high on my list. But I knew that to get better, I had to discipline that part of my brain.

My Football Vision

Now, I never made it to the National Football League. It was never a personal goal of mine and playing that level was not on my radar.

My main vision in high school, like every other kid, was to win the state championship. I went to a school that has always been known for success. I was an offensive lineman at Jackson Prep from 1974 to 1977. I was named by the statewide paper as the top offensive lineman in the state and was honorable mention All-American.

My high school coach was Buddy Crosby, who won the state title six times. When he retired, his record was 109-18, winning 85.2 percent of the time. He always had great teams.

Coach Crosby worked the wimp out of us, and we won.

My junior year at Jackson Prep, I had knee surgery and missed most of that season. The team went 6-4 that year, the worst season since the first year the school opened. I went to the coach at the end of the season and told him, "I can assure you we will never have that record again" and asked his permission to let the senior leadership address the team.

I wanted to have certain demands put on the sophomores, juniors, and now the seniors in accountability. At the weight room, we would all weigh in and out and post our lifting. We'd crack the whip if they missed practice and training. But it made us a better team.

We went 10-1 the next year, with one loss caused by a blocked punt, and won the Conference Championship.

My senior year, I got all these letters from different schools and was recruited by Bear Bryant at the University of Alabama. My brother and sister both went to Alabama.

But I ended up committing to Steve Sloan at Ole Miss in Oxford, Mississippi.

I found out later that Bear Bryant had scheduled a flight to come visit me, and I know when Bear Bryant walks into your living room, you commit. But when he found out I had already committed to Steve Sloan, who was a former quarterback of his, he backed off.

I was one of Coach Sloan's first recruits. He had taken the Ole Miss job on a Wednesday, then called me on a Thursday and they offered me a full scholarship.

My Vision in Life

I always have to have something that drives me.

I was very proud to accomplish a long-time goal before my dad passed away. My wife, Darnell, and I were able to build a building at the African Bible College in Malawi, Africa, named the Spence Dye School of Business and Community Development.

The mission of the college is to train young leaders to inspire their communities to produce responsible citizens, train new leaders, and give back to society to give impoverished citizens an opportunity for education and an opportunity to do something with their lives.

Before Dad died, I was able to share that we would be constructing a building to honor him and his leadership values on that campus. Although he was in and out of dementia then, I could tell he understood because he choked up. He was honored by it. It was such a blessing to be able to share that with him.

The college produced a video about Spence Dye, explaining that he:

"... Grew up, became a great Christian businessman in the town of Jackson, Mississippi. He and his son have been great contributors to the Christian community. That's exactly the kind of Christian businessmen that we need in Malawi. We need Christians who are successful in business so they can give back to the church and give back to mission work. We want our graduates to be a light in the business world and let people know what hard working, honest industrious Christian businessmen are like. That's what we are producing."

It is important to make a difference.

It kind of goes back to where Spence Dye came from and his story of helping people out who need a hand up. To do something like that in America, his story might have just disappeared. But to do it in a place like Africa, where many people need a hand-up along with an education, is something that will live on for a long time.

In my opinion, every goal should be so high, you can barely achieve it. You should have to work hard for it, or you've barely had a goal at all. If you achieve it too easily, you didn't set the bar high enough. If it doesn't scare you, it's not high enough.

In working toward your goal, you have to ignore the doubters. You must run from negativity. Sometimes you must accept reality. Maybe your goal wasn't realistic, and you must adjust it.

If you make a mistake, you learn from that mistake. If you are victorious, you learn from your victory.

Goals let us know where we are going. It's like they say in *Alice in Wonderland*, "If you don't know where you are going, how will you know when you get there?"

You have got to go somewhere. You can't just wander aimlessly in life. Faith is what has kept me going at times.

There was one time I did business with somebody who took a lot of money from me. I was just starting out in business, and my wife and I were expecting our first child. There was no money coming in and I had just received a bill for $428. I had no money to pay for it. I was scared. I didn't even know if I was in the right line of work. But God made it clear for me to continue.

The next day, I got a check in the mail and there were just a few dollars left over, once I paid the bill. That was a confirmation moment to stop feeling sorry for myself.

At our office, Dye Resource Management, we all set goals. My son, Gary, sets his goals. Our office manager, Mandy, sets her goals, and I'll set mine. We have a team goal.

We start every Monday morning with a prayer—to focus on what's best from our clients' standpoint and to give proper advice. We want to represent our clients' interests—not our own. And, if income comes from this, that's good—but our main goal is to help people.

Dad taught me to focus, and my mom taught me to execute my vision and goals. She taught me to do my best and be happy with my best.

I drive myself hard and I always learn from the failures and the successes.

And when our clients win—that is our ultimate goal.

What is Your Goal?

There are some people who may not have any goals—you ask them, "What did you do today? What did you accomplish?" And the answer is, "Not much."

When a man goes into a nursing home, he may only live another year or two. When a woman goes into a nursing home, she may live five to ten more years. I think that's because women are more social.

In past generations, men were often raised to be the breadwinner. That has obviously changed in later generations, where both spouses usually work, but the people who are in nursing homes now are of that older generation. So, a man going into a nursing home may feel he no longer has an identity or purpose. A female may be more comfortable socializing and accepting their new reality.

You must ask yourself, what if I can no longer pursue my goals or vision when I retire, what am I going to do that will stimulate me? Most people will not just go and sit down in a chair but will jump into charity work or become the best gardener, or golfer, or travel to as many countries as they can.

How do you get a vision when you don't have one?

How do you get that drive back?

I have not yet experienced that, but I can say when my football days were over, it was a culmination of a vision. It was great, but eventually, you have got to learn to put the past in the past.

People will still bring my football days up to me, which is wonderful, but it is my past life. I shifted my focus long ago to think about where I am going now.

When I started working in the financial services industry, I found new goals and visions for my business. They just kind of came to me. I didn't sit down and make up a bunch of things that I wanted to do. These were things that would come into my mind strongly, almost like being told.

I've tried to set up a strategic planning alliance, sending and receiving referrals to and from other professionals, such as attorneys and bankers, who could be of assistance to clients. This is beneficial for everyone involved, like when your cardiologist works with your neurologist and the neurologist works with the internal medicine guy. Everybody works together.

I want to be able to provide clients objective opinions, with professionals looking over their shoulder and sitting on the same side of the table.

This is the difference between what I do and a stockbroker who just sells stocks, a banker who pushes their own bank's products, and insurance guys who sell only insurance. That's not a truly objective process for the client. At our firm, we offer both insurance and investment products and strategies are part of a holistic view of our clients' finances.

Doing business this way helps the client, and in turn, leads to more referrals coming through my door because they've heard from family and friends who had a pleasant experience in my office.

TEAMWORK—Then and Now

Whether you're on a football team or just going through life in general, I believe everybody should have a "huddle"—the people who are on your team—men, women, your friends, and family.

These are the people you can count on when the chips are down.

You can look into their eyes and see determination or frustration because they are having a rough time with their opponent. You might see fright or anger, but the most successful people in the huddle are those who have a calmness about them.

I'm fortunate that the huddle in our office is made up of winners, fighters, and overachievers. One team member grew up poor and lived on her floor alone in an apartment, and now is the hardest worker I've ever been associated with.

When clients come in to see us, we are the huddle they're entrusting with their financial futures. Looking into a client's eyes, maybe we'll see things they necessarily don't want to open up, talk about, or share. Maybe they are embarrassed about not being responsible with their finances. They want to get it fixed, but not talk about.

Maybe one spouse wants to talk about the money, the other doesn't. Or they don't want to think about or plan for what would happen if a spouse passed away.

There are a lot of things when you are meeting with clients; it is always a different huddle and there are always different ways to get to the same common goal.

It's all about knowing how to address the issues, read the people, and see what their goals are so you can lead them to that. When you call a huddle, you have to be ready to call a play and change it based on what the client needs.

CHAPTER 4

Coaching and Being Accountable

When my son started playing Little League sports, he wanted me to coach, and I absolutely loved it. That's the ultimate purity of the sport. You have raw talent that needs to be worked, trained, and encouraged.

My son and I had an understanding that, as the coach, if there was ever a choice between him, or another boy of equal talent, becoming a starter, the other kid would get the nod. The last thing I wanted was to have another parent questioning whether I started my son over somebody else.

I told him that meant he had to be that much better than the next person. I can't say he loved the idea, but he understood it.

When you coach, you look for the best qualities in a player and bring them forward. In business, we look for opportunities to do that for our clients.

Everyone has a person who has deeply affected their life. It may be a coach or teacher who worked with you and get the most out of you. They may push you beyond your comfort zone. They may force you to do things you don't want to do to get better.

You get a sense they are doing it because they truly care about you. They can see a value in you, which gives you a feeling of worth. It means a lot when someone you respect is willing to invest their time and energy to push you.

For me, that was Miss Wilder, my eighth-grade English teacher. She was one of the toughest teachers I ever had. As a senior, we were required to go back and take her English class before we could graduate from high school.

She was a very firm, tough lady who demanded the best. She was a perfectionist and expected us to meet her standards.

The last time I saw Miss Wilder was before she passed away. I saw her twenty-five years after my graduation at a restaurant. She saw me and came up to me. I thought she was going to make me diagram a sentence or something. But she came over to tell me hello. I gave her a hug and told her how much I appreciated her. She smiled.

Miss Wilder was the Bear Bryant of teachers. She got the most out of me, and I always appreciated and respected that.

Sometimes these character traits are used in dealing with clients. Some people respond well to tough love. You need to be strong and firm in your decisions. For others, they need someone who is understanding. I have learned which ones need to be pushed and which ones need to be treated a little nicer.

The teachers and coaches I had growing up taught me a work ethic and how to prepare for every detail, through discipline, structure, presentation, and making that extra phone call.

In one case, we had been working with a client regarding a problem for about nine months. He was fighting an insurance company that basically had given him false information. I remained calm. The client was fine with their information, but he didn't know it was false. He assumed it was the truth.

He was going to let the insurance company go without any qualms. I kept telling him to let me work on it. I spent months fighting for this case. It did not look or feel right.

I want to make it clear I did not make a dime on this—not one penny. But I kept calling on the behalf of my clients. I told them to have faith and patience.

Our office argued with the insurance company back and forth. Over time, we finally got the information I needed and proved the insurance company was wrong.

I called him into the office and laid out all the papers for him on a twelve-foot conference table of everything in chronological order. This is what we do business for. I'm very proud that we were able to help our client. We were able to do something for him and his family.

Sometimes the insurance companies are right, and we accept that. But sometimes they are wrong, and that's when we strive to achieve the best outcome for our clients.

To me, that is the offensive lineman mentality—a success is a touchdown scored. I like knowing it was done quietly. There won't be any headlines to read about it.

Accountability

All my life, I've learned to be accountable—both in my personal life and my business.

As I mentioned at the start of this book (and in its title), my family has always been proud of who we are. We have always been a close-knit family.

We have a saying at my home with our children, "We are the Dyes, we stick together, friends forever. I love you."

Now, both kids are both grown and married, but they know we will always be friends and we love each other.

That, to me, is accountability.

Having my parents in town gave my children an extra layer of accountability while growing up. From generation to generation, we passed down the mantra, "Don't ruin the family name."

We hope this same level of accountability goes with the name on our door.

Little kids pick someone to look up to—maybe it's an athlete or Miss America. Over the years, I've tried to pick mentors I could observe and learn from—things like signs of character, integrity, knowledge, and wisdom.

For instance, my insurance mentor was an extremely disciplined person. I worked under him for about five years, and we have a lot of mutual respect. I didn't become him, but I learned from him. I went in with very little knowledge, but I came out mentally tougher and stronger.

I have the heart and desire to grow and push and drive, but some people can help me do better.

So, if you want to learn to fly, hang around eagles.

Ted Engstrom, in his book, "The Pursuit of Excellence" tells a story of an eagle egg being placed in a nest of prairie chicken eggs.

The eaglet hatched with the brood of chicks and grew up with them.

The changeling eagle thought he was a prairie chicken. He forever did what they did, scratching the ground for seeds and insects to eat. He tried to fit in.

"He clucked and cackled. And he flew in a brief thrashing of wings and flurry of feathers no more than a few feet off the ground."

That's what prairie chickens did.

Years passed and the eagle grew old.

"One day, he saw a magnificent bird far above him in a cloudless sky—it soared with scarcely a beat of its strong golden wings.

"That's an eagle," a neighboring prairie chicken clucked. "You could never be like him."

The eagle—raised as a prairie chicken—never realized its full potential.

So, how does that relate to finance? This way of thinking allows me to see financial problems, objections, or concerns from every different angle.

We do not represent one company. We represent hundreds of opportunities for our clients. A lot of our competitors will work for one company, which limits what they can offer their clients.

We are independent. We are not going to take your size twelve foot and put it in a size nine shoe and tell you, "Hey, that feels good!"

We can tailor-fit solutions to your specific needs.

We are not beholding to any one company that is dictating what we need to do or what we need to sell our clients.

I tell my clients that I represent them. My priority is to find strategies and products that work for their needs, not the needs of an insurance company, or an annuity, or financial company. I have thousands of employers—my clients—who I answer to. My job is to make all those "employers" happy. If you work for a company that dictates that you can only write a certain product, you're doing a disservice to your clients.

The industry has changed tremendously. Back in the 1980s, you could write with one financial company and pretty much take care of all your clients' needs. Over the past forty years, industries have changed. Certain companies specialize in certain areas.

We work for you. We want to take the time to sit down to get to know you and find out your whole story. We take a lot of pride in being independent.

When you become our client, it's not purely a transactional process. We stay in touch with you. I send out birthday cards to all my clients and a Christmas letter. It's more of a personal relationship.

How we help our clients with their money is the same way we choose to manage our own.

I, by nature, am not a big risk-taker with my money. I strategically design my retirement income strategies to help reduce losses and capitalize on guaranteed growth opportunities via fixed insurance products and strategies.

Don't get me wrong. I am not opposed to market risk for younger people or for those people who don't mind high risk. That's their choice. It's just not our intention to chase market returns and run the risk of major losses prior to retirement. Our clients are typically looking for reasonable growth based on protection of their money.

I ask people, "If you made $100,000 on the market today, would it change your lifestyle?"

Most answer no. But if you lost 25 to 50 percent of your savings in the market, would it affect your retirement plans and bother you?

If the answer is yes, then you are probably a good fit for us. If you are not bothered by market losses and can afford those losses, then I might refer you to a stockbroker who can better assist your needs.

There's nothing wrong with this, it's just not our strategy. We focus on protecting the right portion of your money from market risk and loss, typically for those in or nearing retirement.

We explain to people a concept that is often overlooked: If you had $1 million in the market and lost 40 percent, as in 2008, then your value is now $600,000. If you earned 40 percent the next day, you are only earning 40 percent on $600,000. Now your investment is still only $840,000, still $160,000 short of your original $1 million.

In other words, it can take years to recover your losses.

The insurance solutions we offer are principally protected. That means that in a down market, your "worst case" return would be a zero return—no loss of any principal. This is a safety feature, especially for those approaching or already in retirement.

Plus, when the market rebounds, you can be rebounding with $1 million, not $600,000. Be smart with your money for retirement. Be less stressed financially.

Our mission statement is:

We offer a path to financial independence. Being financially independent means having options to conduct one's lifestyle relatively free of economic considerations. This is approached by utilizing organized and wisely thought-out insurance strategies using proper risk management.

We believe in giving our clients the opportunity and tools that can help them live their lives free from financial struggles, knowing their family will always be provided for. We divide income into two areas: one for responsibilities and one for recreation. Your "responsible" needs are things like basic living expenses, and "recreation" is for enjoying life and doing the things you have always dreamed of doing after you've set enough aside to care for your basic responsibilities.

So, our philosophy is to let us help you create a safety net. We help you manage risk. We have life insurance in case you don't live long enough to get to reach your dream—the life insurance can help fulfill those needs for your family.

Most importantly, we are with you through every step of your retirement.

Several decades ago, my dad and I had an agreement when he was watching his parents suffer from dementia. He said he wanted people to remember him the way he was.

He was very personable. He knew everybody. And, he said, when he got to the point of dementia, he wanted me to put him in a nursing home. "I want you to agree with me, with a handshake, that you put me in, then turn around, walk away, and don't come back."

Easier said than done. Instead, my approach is to take a tough thing and do what I can to turn it good.

That's the same goal I aim to apply in my work with our clients. We're dealing with real people, real lives, real dreams, and real goals. That's what gives us our passion to work with clients and help them through the rough roads.

The whole objective of any professional in any profession is this: how can you assist people in ways to help them live life better?

CHAPTER 5

The Power of Faith in Business

I didn't become a Christian until my senior year in college. At the time, I was considering a career like ministry, but more like marriage and family counseling. I was unsure what I was going to do. With that said, I earned my insurance license in 1981, while I was still in college.

I was moving toward the insurance business, but not sure yet. I worked on the youth staff at our local church, The First Presbyterian Church of Jackson, and after six months of soul-searching, the Lord made it clear to me that I was to go into business. A lot of things were happening then to me. Some doors opened while others closed.

It happened enough times that it made sense for me to go forward in business.

I remember a time when I was twenty-two years old and we were down in Fairhope, Alabama, at the Grand Hotel. It was a business meeting with all these guys who were much older than me. They were sitting around at dinner. They were all talking about ways insurance can be structured and sold to make more money.

I remember being really disenchanted and disappointed because these were people that, as a young man, I was supposed to look up to and respect. I was there to learn from them, but they seemed more interested in generating commissions for themselves than the best interest of their clients.

I left there and went back to my room. I was struggling. I opened up the Bible and turned to Psalms 37:1-9:

"Do not fret because of evil men or be envious of those who do wrong;

For like the grass they will soon wither, like green plants they will soon die away.

Trust in the LORD and do good; dwell in the land and enjoy safe pasture.

Delight yourself in the LORD and he will give you the desires of your heart.

Commit your way to the LORD; trust in him and he will do this:

He will make your righteousness shine like the dawn, the justice of your case like the noonday sun.

Be still before the LORD and wait patiently for him; do not fret when men succeed

In their ways, when they carry out their wicked schemes.

Refrain from anger and turn from wrath; do not fret—it leads only to evil.

For evil men will be cut off, but those who hope in the LORD will inherit the land."

I interpreted it as, "Simply leave them to their own ways."

All those people have pretty much disappeared now. Most of them had to get out of business—they didn't last. One guy went to prison for theft.

About that same time, in 1981, the movie *Chariots of Fire* came out. It was about runners from Great Britain who were training for the 1924 Olympics in Paris. Eric Liddell, played by Ian Charleson, was a devout Christian son of Scottish missionaries. I loved the part when Eric's sister approaches him and tells him he is taking his running too seriously and that the family wants him to concentrate more on being a missionary.

Eric makes the comment, "When I run, I feel God's pleasure."

That is what I do. When I do my business and I do it right, it's not about me. It's not about how much am I going to make.

I believe if you are doing what you are supposed to be doing—instead of it being a job—you do it because you feel God's pleasure.

That is my belief, and it is reflected in our business logo. Our Dye company logo is similar to the Olympic torch, which signifies the *Chariots of Fire* theme.

It goes back to Isaiah 40:31:

"But those who hope in the Lord will renew their strength. They will soar on wings like eagles; they will run and not grow weary; they will walk and not be faint."

It means you can continue to thrive and move forward, and God will sustain you.

That *Chariots of Fire* movie resonated with me—to the point that we will never do any business on Sundays. That's a strict rule in our office. No business is talked about, no emails are read or sent, or even thought about on Sunday. We just don't do that.

We will respond to emails and requests on Saturdays. We don't mind that. We will respond every other day of the week, but Sundays are strictly off-limits.

If someone comes up to me at church on Sunday and has a business question, I tell them I won't talk to them about that right now, but I will call them tomorrow. And I do follow up with them.

But think about that thought: "When I run, I feel God's pleasure." What a great mentality. What a great thought in whatever you do, whether it is your work, your family, your hobby, or something that you have a gift for and truly enjoy doing.

In my spare time, I enjoy hunting and golfing. There is a place I go to in Colorado where I tell my wife, that when I am there, I go to touch the face of God. It is there that I get away from everything.

There are a lot of neat things that have happened to me out there spiritually and emotionally.

Whatever you do, if you feel God's pleasure, that should be enough. That's what drew me into my business.

People ask, "Where do you get all your business from?"

I don't ask for referrals. It just comes. Now, that doesn't mean I sit and wait for people to knock on my door. I work, but as a result of the labor, good things happen.

You have to have faith—and that's not easy all the time.

HUDDLE UP!

Our nation is, at times, very divided. Keep in mind, I grew up in the South during the 1960s.

I made one of my first friends when I was in first grade in Louisville, Kentucky. He was a black guy. Nobody else would talk to him. I didn't care. We played together. His name was Martin.

In my late teens, I worked on the loading docks of Western Auto in Jackson, where we loaded eighteen-wheelers. I was the only white guy.

On the loading docks, I learned a lot there about work ethic, what I wanted to be in life, and about the loyalties of friendship.

I still have the friends I made on the loading docks decades ago. The experiences I have shared with these men were life-changing. Those guys took me under their wings and were really good friends to me. They treated me as one of their own.

They would ask me to go out to places with them at night, and I did.

Let me tell you, when you were white in an all-black bar after midnight in Jackson, Mississippi, in the 1970s, you kind of stood out, especially if you had a cowboy hat on. I didn't think anything of it. These other guys would come over and ask me what I was doing there, and my guys would stand up for me. They were protective. They were and remain good friends.

In life, some friends may drift in and out of your life, but some will stay. Now, there are some people on Facebook I might disagree with politically. I've had people tell me, "Dye, if you ever run for office, I will stand behind you 100 percent because I know where your heart is and I know you are a good man."

Even though we might disagree, it does not hinder our friendship.

I believe anybody has the right to believe and vote their conscience. My uncle died in the Battle of the Bulge for you to have that right. I don't have a problem with people who disagree.

I respect that.

If everybody were Republicans, we'd be in trouble. If everybody were Democrats, we'd be in trouble. It's really both sides keeping checks and balances that keeps us in line.

I respect the fact that people have differing opinions.

Not long ago, I reached out to a friend from Mississippi. He is a black man who played football for Ole Miss. He's a lot younger than I am. We came together and I said, "You know what, we don't have riots in Mississippi . . . Of all the places in this country, you'd think Mississippi would be the target for race relations because we have such a horrible reputation."

He laughed and said the last thing he ever would have thought was that he would be sitting down with an old guy with a white beard talking about race relations.

But he's like my brother now. We see each other and give each other big hugs. He's a big strong guy playing the pros. When it comes to politics, at the core of either side, there are good people trying to bring others together. Let's find a common ground and not be stereotyped as the white guy or the black guy.

The friendships I have in the past and now reflect some of the most loving, generous, and kind people I have ever met.

I believe I can help bring different generations and races together. We can find common ground—a love of family and faith. Let's just move forward and show unity.

We have all made mistakes, but I also think Mississippi could be a wonderful place to start bringing people together.

I want to do it because it is the right thing. I want to help provide sound financial guidance to minorities who are under-represented. I think we need to bring people together, find unity, and create a dialogue.

It is about sitting down and talking things through—finding out the needs of one another, instead of sitting on the sidelines like everybody else does.

Let's diagnose the problem before we try to fix it.

If we can do those kinds of things, I think we can be a better community, state, and country.

A great example of this is athletes working together. They bleed, they sweat together. They've grown up together. They sacrifice what they want to do together. And they've picked each other up when they get knocked down. I don't care what color you are if we are going toward one common goal.

One thing I have always enjoyed being involved with is prison ministry. I used to go to prisons and speak to inmates. I don't know why, but these guys resonate with me. What I love about them is that you can speak frankly, hit them right between the eyes, and they love it. You can call it the way you see it. They like talking direct, and I like that.

I find it's the same with athletes. They like directness. Let's just put things out on the table and deal with it. That's how you make progress.

Finding Your Own Gift from God

I've had people come to me and say they don't know what their gift is—what their skill set is.

I tell them to do something that was very beneficial to me. It is an action meant to be confidential and private. Take maybe ten people, (it's fine if you don't have that many) who you really know, trust, and love. It could be your spouse, your parents, or close friends. It could be anybody you feel led to go to.

Ask them, in all seriousness, what is it that you see in me that you like? What are the qualities? When you do that survey, see if there is a common thread. Ask them to write it down.

They may tell you ten different things, or just one or two— but there is always going to be a common thread. I tell people that is your unique ability, that's your God-given gift. That's what people see in you universally. So, when you meet with a client or a person for the first time, this is what others see in you.

You can build a business or career around your unique gift.

Michael Jordan said, "Limits, like fear, are often just an illusion." People, in general, are very content with mediocrity. But to find a gift, your gift, means you are doing what comes naturally to you. So, when you are working, you almost feel guilty because it is so easy. It's "feeling God's pleasure." It's more fun.

Jerry Jeff Walker, the country music and folk singer, used to say that playing country music is getting paid for something I'd be doing anyway.

That's how it feels when you find your unique gift. You can build your business and life around that. You are doing something that comes naturally to you.

But so many times when you are growing up, especially playing sports, you are taught to work on your weaknesses. You find out the areas you are weak in, and you work on those to make yourself stronger. In business, you find out what your strengths are, and you make those stronger. You take your weaknesses, and you hire people who have those areas as their strengths. I don't want a bunch of strong weaknesses.

I want to be good at what I do. I want the people I hire to be strong at what they do.

To go beyond mediocrity, you must scare yourself and get big. If your goal doesn't scare you, it isn't big enough. To get bigger, you've got to ignore the doubters. You have to know what your vision is. You must stay above the limiting mindset that says you have gotten too big. Your success is limited only by your brain and the fears of success—and the fear of failure.

I encourage people to think a certain way.

Your fears of failure and even your fears of success are debilitating. Thomas Edison said, "I have not failed, not once. I have found 10,000 ways that do not work."

There is no such thing as failure.

The only thing that is failure is the failure to try. If you try and it didn't work, it is not a failure. You must find a better way to make it work.

A growth mentality is what makes life fun to me. It is a reason to move forward.

If I set a goal, I achieve it every time. I see it. I face it every day. I do what I need to do to get there.

I love encouraging people to do the same.   I love encouraging them to help set a goal. But they have to be the ones who set it. I can't set it for them.

But I can help them pave the road to do it, and I will hold them accountable.

CHAPTER 6

Doing Old-School Business in a Modern World

In a world where everything is so fast-paced and quick, at our office we still do some things the old-fashioned way.

We send out birthday cards to clients. We write Christmas letters. It is the type of thing almost nobody does anymore.

Most people may wander through social media, thinking that's how you stay in touch. For me, it's like the huddle-up mentality of football. People may think they don't need to huddle up anymore, but the needs are even greater than before.

In our society, the needs of people are ever-changing, and the personal touch is just as important as ever.

We like to do things personal, based on an individual's needs. Sometimes it's good to get back to basics rather than doing things the quick and easy way.

In my line of work, I often get questions from people about what they should do with their money. That's why the personal touch, rather than a cookie-cutter approach, is still so very important.

The Right Insurance Can Add to Your Own Wealth

When it comes to financial planning, some of the most frequently asked questions are who should get life insurance and when.

It is too late if you have become medically uninsurable. Simply put, if you are uninsurable, you can't get life insurance at reasonable rates, if at all.

That's why when you are younger, it just makes more financial sense to get it. You should definitely have it if you are married and if you are planning on having children.

Sometimes single people will get it in their twenties, only if they have a health risk and they need to get it now to ensure their insurability on down the road—so that when they do have a spouse and children, they still have the insurance to help provide for loved ones when they are gone.

Usually, when young couples are starting out, there may be some early financial struggles that make it hard to pay for life insurance. But when a couple starts having children, it becomes more important in case something were to happen to either parent.

For most people, you need life insurance to replace lost income when you die. I've had people tell me when it comes to life insurance, I make the complicated easy.

People view life insurance as a negative for how it is sold, often using high-pressure sales. I tell many of my clients, especially the younger ones, to purchase term insurance if they need coverage but have limited funds. It's generally the least expensive way to do insurance planning. If you die tomorrow, your spouse won't care if it's term or permanent. What will matter is how much, and a $2 million term policy can be sold for less than say a $200,000 permanent policy.

I say the difference between term and permanent insurance is like paying rent versus a mortgage. You are going to rent it for a while. You won't be building up any equity, but you'll have a roof over your head. Over time, that rent is going to go up and up and you haven't built up any equity. That's when having permanent insurance is more like buying a home. You are going to be paying more for it, but you are building up equity. Over time and if you fund it properly, you may have respectful cash value built up as you have paid in premiums.

On Annuities, Death, and Why Saving is So Important

I'm going to state the obvious: from a planning standpoint, postmortem is a bit late for financial advice. But when one of our clients dies, we help organize the necessary information to help put their affairs together.

The surviving spouse is often the female. We meet with them, go through all the information, and work with them on how to manage their finances if they choose. I try to tell them to not make any major decisions for maybe the next six months. Let the money just sit in the bank for a while. Let the dust settle. There is a grieving process.

What we see after the death of a spouse is that the surviving spouse often goes into a fog. People are coming into their house from every direction. The spouse is in shock trying to figure out what needs to be done. A lot of times, the person who passed away was the one controlling the finances and managing everything.

The surviving spouse then starts to panic and think about what they need to do immediately. They start to feel like they are fumbling the ball. They ask, "What am I supposed to be doing right now that I'm not?" A lot of times, they don't need to do a thing.

They always ask how they will survive. Where's the money going to come from? What do we have? What don't we have?

You see this across the board. A lot of times, the person who doesn't handle the books, so to speak, has no clue what somebody has or doesn't have.

We had a well-respected man in town who had been a very successful businessman and died of cancer. After his death, his wife contacted me for advice. He was not a client, but she shared with me his information, and he had nothing.

His wife was roughly sixty years old with five children. They were all grown, but she had to go live with them. She had no way to grow an income.

She thought they were very well off. It was amazing her husband left nothing for his family.

I call this "willful ignorance." Sometimes people don't want to know how bad off they are.

People will often ask us to help do a financial evaluation. But you'll notice that after a while, they are either very hesitant or some of them simply don't want to know. Some are embarrassed. They know they are in bad shape, and they don't want to admit it.

It's like if somebody has cancer and they don't want to admit it. They ignore it and hope it might go away. But once they pass away, your spouse and family are left exposed.

I've found people who make good incomes may have this willful ignorance. They are working hard every day, but don't take time to gather financial information. A good planner can pull together a team of people that can help them. They will complain about a $1,500 legal fee to do a will, even if it might save them $50,000 in the long run.

Tips for a Solid Financial Foundation

When it comes to annuities, there are several different types on the market, some better than others, in my experience. Some have higher fees and it may be difficult to understand all of their costs. Others are designed to die when you die. There are hundreds of annuities out there. Some companies may have ten different annuity products. Some may have one or two.

But a properly designed annuity can be an effective tool to help someone in their retirement age, where they can have a guaranteed income stream for life.

We often recommend fixed indexed annuities, which allow you to earn interest tied to an external market index, but with no risk due to market loss, since your money is never invested in the market itself.

For example, if you purchased a fixed index with $100,000 and the index gain the following year (adjusted for limitations often called a cap or spread) resulted in a 10% interest credit, then $110,000 is your new floor. You can't go below that number. So, if you had $110,000 in 2008 and the market crashed, you still had $110,000. You don't lose a penny. You also didn't make a penny during those down years, but you had zero percent return.

Think about how some people lost up to 30 to 50 percent of their assets in their portfolios during 2008, depending on what their risks were or how high they were into the stocks.

But one big benefit of an annuity is that it grows tax-deferred, so you don't pay taxes until you make a withdrawal. At that time you'll pay ordinary income taxes, as well as a 10 percent federal penalty if you're under age fifty-nine and a half, so annuities are definitely long-term income vehicles. An annuity also offers you guaranteed income for the rest of your life. So, at age seventy, the right annuity can trigger an income stream for the rest of your life. Let's say the annuity pays you $50,000 annually for the rest of your life.

Your other income sources may be designed to run out by the time you reach eighty-eight or eighty-nine years old. But with the right annuity, you can continue to receive a lifetime income, even if you live to be 120 years old.

Many people like the stability of an annuity. They like knowing that when they die, their spouse can continue to receive an annuity income.

A lot of people worry about retirement and if they will outlive their money.

This is where I ask, "How much income do you need?"

If we decide that an annuity is a good fit for your income plan, we can determine up front how much you need to put into an annuity to provide you an income stream that can last as long as you do.

Some annuities have a long-term care benefit plan, called an income doubler. For example, if you are drawing $50,000 a year in income, it will double to $100,000 a year for up to five years, then go back to $50,000 if you are have specific qualified long-term care needs.

People who aren't overly familiar with finances may feel like they have this mountain they must climb, and they are sitting at the bottom. They may feel like they are never going to climb or grow.

In our seminars, we use an analogy of a guy standing in a suit at the base of the mountain. He is not dressed or prepared to climb that mountain.

The stock market can appeal to the risk-takers because it provides the possibility to climb the mountain quicker, but if they fall, it can be a dramatic and long tumble.

Others choose to participate in the market more conservatively. Individuals who have a fixed or fixed index annuity can climb, and each time they do, they are locked in. There is never a risk of market loss.

If you don't have the proper financial foundation and the stock market crashes, you may have already retired and find you don't have enough money to live on. Timing is everything, and we can help guide you.

CHAPTER 7

Finding Your Financial Journey From Retirement to Death to Beyond

The people I personally enjoy working with most are those who truly need help.

Obviously, some people come to us who have done well financially, and we help them, too.

For instance, if someone comes to us with $20 million in assets and savings, they are going to be fine. They will get through their retirement.

But I feel our biggest impact comes from helping those who are trying to do well and need a leg up—or maybe it is people who have done well, understand the value of the dollar, and just need guidance on maintaining what they already have.

Money is not something they have simply inherited. They have worked for it, were wise stewards, and have tried to do the right things in life.

We try to protect people from losing money—that's where our passion is and the core of our business.

We've been there. My dad was there. Remember, I am only one generation removed from poverty.

When I grew up, my parents put us in good schools. I didn't care if my classmates had more than I did because our family had core values. Family was everything. Not material goods.

The message I was given by my family was to be nice to everybody—from the janitor to the CEO.

I prefer to help people who are humble and almost apologetic because they think they don't have enough money. Those are the ones I feel we can help the most.

I don't care how much money you have or don't have. My dad instilled in us that everybody is important, regardless of their social stature.

In our office, people often come to us with a variety of questions.

Should they get long-term care? How do they care for parents with dementia? How do they pay for the unforeseen?

Aging is hard. It is personal. No one really has a blueprint for what to do in all circumstances. But as people near retirement, these questions become more critical to answer.

What we learned is there really wasn't much information out there to help guide people through these things. We take each of these situations, learn from them, and help people so they don't have to plow the same field that we already plowed.

What I have seen with a lot of clients is that they don't take long-term care seriously until they must deal with it with their own parents. Then, it becomes more of a reality, and they look at their own lives and take assessment. They ask, "Could this happen to me? And is this what I want?"

There is no one cookie-cutter solution.

Some people will say they will take care of their parents or spouse. Others will write a check to have someone else take care of their loved one. What a person does when it comes time to take care of a loved one is all over the chart.

It's about the relationships you have. If that person has dementia, it becomes personal as to how you talk with them.

Sometimes, you must play along to make things go smoothly. You can't say: "Dad, you aren't making any sense" or "Dad, you've already said this to me five times today."

It does nothing but hurt feelings and frustrate them.

Someone once said to me, "What does it matter, he probably doesn't know who you are anymore."

Doesn't matter? My dad or mom may not remember who I am, but I remember them!

That's the reason I take care of them.

When you are a client, we will go through a series of discussions on a range of topics, such as the health care directive and how to handle it. We make recommendations about gathering financial information and what to do with a brother or sister who is nonresponsive to your requests.

How do you get other family members involved?

When do you put your loved one in a nursing home?

Or even when you go out to dinner, should you take a change of pants and other items along? (And yes, you should.)

We do things like helping you learn how to put your name on the checking account so if that person dies, you have access to their checking account to pay bills. It seems as if almost everybody has to deal with these types of issues. It can be costly if you don't plan accordingly.

My uncle gave me this advice: "Bobby, you can go to your parents' house and stay twenty-four hours, seven days a week, but it is never going to be enough."

He went on to say, "Do not allow yourself to get on a guilt trip, because your mother is going to want you to stay there—she's never going to want you to leave. And when you do leave, you will feel guilty. It will never be enough. Just do what you need to do, then go. Don't allow yourself to get pulled down."

That was the best advice I was given.

Sometimes people have come to us and asked, "What if we don't have enough money to care for them?"

That is a real concern.

But sometimes, there is nothing else you can do but buckle down and take them in. You may have children and they also need to be involved in those conversations.

Some will quit their job and stay home to help; others will involve their friends, church, and whomever else to step in. But this is the kind of thing that can blow your own retirement, and that's where planning for long-term care comes in.

It is essential to plan in advance. I truly think that to have a solid financial foundation, it is a matter of education. You know, when you are in your twenties, you are ten feet tall and bulletproof. Mortality is not on your radar. You haven't lost friends. You haven't seen people die.

But by the time you get to your sixties, you have lost friends, you've seen parents of friends pass, if not your own parents.

In our office with our clients, we try to educate people about the long haul. We talk about the need for insurance. The truth is life insurance is a need—not a want. You buy it because you love your family.

The following is a list we provide clients who become caregivers, particularly to people with dementia. It's based on what we have discovered as we take care of our own family members.

Long-Term Care

1. Dementia is a disease where you see your parents die twice.
2. Role reversal—you are now the parent; your mom/dad is now the child.
3. When a person has dementia, it is simply best to go along with them, humor them, and tell a little white lie if you must.
4. Let your loved one feel like they are in control, even though they aren't. Let them hold onto their independence—even if it's just in their head—for as long as they can.
   a. People with dementia tend to get fixated on a certain thing—this can last for days/months.
   b. They have no filter on their speech.
   c. Going out to dinner can be difficult, but go when you can. Just be prepared with extra clothing, allow plenty of time, and be patient.
5. Will, Healthcare Directive & Power of Attorney
   a. There can be issues with second marriages and the children of the step-parent.
   b. There should be a unified front, but you shouldn't feel any pressure—you are exercising the will and wishes of your parent.
6. It's best not to have too many cooks in the kitchen. Divide tasks among family members, and make sure everyone's roles are clear cut.
7. Keep updated medication list and emergency phone numbers on fridge.
   a. Most likely, the medicines will constantly change.

8. It is always important to keep the following with you either on your cell phone or in a file: copies of Power of Attorney, insurance cards, photo ID, Social Security card, and a list of updated medications.

9. There comes a point where medications will need to be locked away, so an accidental overdose doesn't occur.

10. With Medicare Part D (the prescription plan), you must enroll every year—you pick the plan that works best for you, your meds, and your pharmacy.

11. Look into VA benefits if applicable.

12. Doctor visits can be frustrating for you and your loved one.
    a. The doctor will address them, and they will answer incorrectly, and you will correct them, and nobody leaves happy.
    b. Taking a prepared list of questions and comments that the doctor can read before they come into the exam room is extremely helpful. (Just give to the nurse as discreetly as possible.)

13. Make sure the doctor's office has YOUR number on file, *not* only your parent's (with their permission, of course!)
    a. It is quite common for the doctor's office to call and leave messages with your loved one, which is not helpful at all!

14. People with dementia tend to wander away from the home—a security system should be in place.

15. UTIs are common among the elderly. Symptoms include confusion, agitation, hallucinations, poor motor skills, dizziness, and falling.

16. It is very important to have a budget in place— know where the money is going.

17. Consider adding yourself to checking/savings accounts and be sure to check bank and credit card statements for unusual charges—people tend to take advantage of the elderly via phone scams.

18. Gather all important documents in one place—statements (checking/savings/other investments), life insurance/long-term care policies, pension plans, etc.

19. Remove all valuables from the house prior to caretakers coming into the home.

20. Car keys will need to be locked away.

21. Put restraints on phone and cable.

22. Get pre-approved for long-term care coverage prior to entering the facility.

23. Alzheimer's does not qualify for hospice care, but a pre-existing condition like heart disease does.

24. Be proactive as far as funeral arrangements—burial/cremation, pallbearers, obituary, suit/dress, etc.

25. Life insurance inheritance can be used to replenish what was spent on long-term care.

JUST REMEMBER:

- You can be there twenty-four/seven and you will still feel like you are not doing enough.
- Don't let anyone make you feel guilty about the time you do or do not spend with your loved one.
- This is a phase; it won't last forever. You are not a victim, and you are not alone. Lots of families go through this very same thing.
- Take care of yourself; make time for yourself and your own immediate family.

We also make these recommendations:

- Make sure all guns are out of the house.
- Be aware of Sundowner's Syndrome—symptoms that occur at night with people with memory loss, causing increased confusion, disorientation, anxiety, and agitation.
- Get your own affairs in order.

And these are the documents you should be able to easily access:

Documentation Guide

Legal Documents:
- Trusts
- Wills
- Estate Planning
- Health Care Directives
- Durable Powers of Attorney

Investments:
- Bank Statements
- CDs
- Annuities
- Mutual Funds
- Stocks, Bonds, etc.
- Retirement Plans: Employer/Personal
- Education Plan Funding

Loan Documents:
- Personal
- Business

Personal Insurance:
- Life
- Disability Income
- Long Term Care
- Medical
- Personal Liability

Property/Casualty Insurance:
- Home
- Auto
- Business
- Worker's Compensation
- Profession Liability

Tax Returns (past two years) Financial Statements:
- Personal
- Business

Real Estate:
- Personal
- Business

Appraisals:
- Personal
- Business

Marriage/Divorce Decrees Funeral Planning:
- Pre-Paid Plans
- Cemetery Deed(s)

Miscellaneous (copies of):
- Driver's License
- Medical Cards
- Birth Records/Death Certificates

- Veteran Administration Benefits
- Credit Cards
- Other Wallet Items, etc.
- Safe Deposit Box Information
- Social Security Card

This is not an all-inclusive list but is to be used as a guide only. Please add any other documents/information as needed below:

_____

_____

_____

_____

_____

_____

_____

_____

Our Experience—The Key is Organization

To date, our office has helped our clients work through more than 120 different death claims. So, our experience is very in-depth. After a client dies, we typically meet with the spouse and help them figure out where everything is.

We caution them to not feel any pressure, don't make any big decisions, don't let family members pressure you into deciding anything.

We also let them know that life insurance companies don't come looking for you. If you don't file a claim, they just don't pay. So, what we try to do is sit down and help the surviving spouse organize things. A lot of times, family members want to close things down—and it can become a money grab.

Without proper planning, families can quickly get crossways with each other.

Picture if you die and you leave everything to your spouse, and they have no idea where everything is. Of course, you know where everything is, but you haven't pulled it together.

Think about the person you are leaving it to.

The biggest criteria I tell people is to get your information organized so people can access it. We will sit down and walk your survivors through the process, whether it is contacting their other advisors or working with the attorneys.

The important thing is for you to list who your most trusted advisors are.

People often don't do this type of organization because they don't see the value in it themselves. But they might do it out of love for their surviving spouse.

Let's say you have a farm, and your son works with you on the farm. You also have a daughter who is married and lives in another town. She owns part of the farm but doesn't work there with you. What can we do to reimburse her appropriately?

There are a lot of things we look at both pre-death and post-death. How can we handle all these issues that are fair to everyone involved?

If you do your pre-planning and sit down with your kids and talk to them, let them know that if something happens to you and/or your spouse, this is what will happen.

So please, organize all your financial information and documents and list your financial advisors. Make it clear in a will how you want your money distributed and what you want to be done.

We often suggest our clients talk to an attorney about a trust, where you can leave a certain amount of money to help your children, grandchildren, and great-grandchildren to achieve the things they want to achieve, as seed money to help them get started.

These are all issues that we can help guide our clients through in creating their own pathways. We are here to help.

CHAPTER 8

Two Types of Checks in Retirement

My goal for when I die is that the very last check I write bounces. This means I've enjoyed all the money I worked hard to earn. (I say figuratively, not literally.) I want clients to enjoy their retirement years and not be obsessed with financial worries.

Most people say they want to save something for their kids. They pass up the opportunity to travel, take that special trip, or get that boat they wanted.

But what often happens? When you die, you leave your money and kids behind, then they buy a boat and take that trip. They do all the things that you wish you'd have done with the money.

The way I'm structured, I want to enjoy and spend every dollar that I have ever earned. My wife and I are going to enjoy all that we have ever earned. We put in the hard work and labor. It comes back into life insurance for the kids. When we pass away, there is nothing to fight over. But you will have life insurance that will pay out tax-free to each one of them.

Most people love that idea. When I do seminars, I can see it resonate with people. People want to do things they have always dreamed of doing—but they don't because they want to leave something to the kids.

As an insurance and retirement income professional, I like to say you have two types of checks: one for your responsibilities and one for recreation. The first covers all the needs you absolutely have to take care of. The rest of your money can then be "play money" for whatever you want to do. I don't care what you do with it—blow it.

My goal is to help you get where you have enough, you can do what you enjoy doing without being financially stressed. You have the money to take care of the mortgage, healthcare, utilities, and whatever you want to do. Anything above and beyond that is fun money.

I always want people to know that a good income strategy is always much more than money. So many times, the focus is always money, money, money. But the focus should be about doing the right thing and taking care of your family.

It's the peace of mind that I was able to give my father when he was passing away and in his last hours. I whispered to him. I said, "Mom is going to be fine. Because of your planning, you did great. It's okay to go. I know you are hanging on because you don't want to leave her. But Dad, Mom is going to be fine, financially. She's going to miss you, but she is still fine, financially. You do not need to worry. It's all been taken care of."

And it was.

To me, it was a blessing to be able to tell my father it was okay. It's not about the money. It's about the peace of mind and the love of family.

It's knowing that you have set up your strategies and been responsible, and that is the blessing to achieve when you get to that point.

Three-Legged Stool of Income

We host a seminar twice a month explaining some of the financial risks that can come up in retirement. We do not give tax, legal, or investment advice.

Many people in their late fifties and early sixties are profiting from the accumulation phase of their financial life, but in retirement, you transition to the distribution phase.

In the first twenty-five to thirty years of a career, people often question how life insurance will come into play if you don't live long enough. But in retirement, people are on the back nine of their life (to use a golf analogy)—and now, the question is what if they live too long? What if YOU live beyond your earning years? How can we manage your money to make it last as long as possible?

When you retire, think of your retirement income as a three-legged stool: income typically streams in from pensions, Social Security, and your personal savings. If you lose one leg of that stool, your retirement plan may be less effective. So, we discuss your personal savings to help you manage that money properly because in our experience, we've seen a lot of people who don't have a great personal savings account.

I tell people to remember that an investment portfolio alone is not a retirement plan.

Everybody always says, "I've got a retirement plan—here are my investments."

That's not a plan.

That's like having gas but no car. It's what makes the car run, but eventually, you will run out of gas if you are not careful.

Most people, when they come in to meet us, really have no clue what insurance options are available to them. Our job is to walk people through it.

We ask, "What do you see as the biggest risks to your retirement savings? What could happen in your retirement years once you fully retire and you are living off your savings income? What is the biggest risk to that nest egg?"

It could be stock market adjustments.

Another big risk to your savings, if you haven't taken precautions, could be long-term care. A long-term health care claim can drain the pot quickly if you don't have a long-term care policy or a strategy to cover those costs.

Pre-Planning for Long-Term Health Care

While we are not estate planning attorneys, we often suggest having a properly designed will designating a healthcare directive and a power of attorney.

If you don't have a will, we recommend you get it done immediately, then designate a power of attorney.

If you're incapacitated and can't make your own decisions, power of attorney gives a spouse, child, or friend the ability to make those decisions on your behalf. They have full control of your estate.

If you have a parent who starts losing their capacities, a power of attorney lets you help take care of them. Without it, it can be difficult to talk with hospitals and doctors about their care.

My father could have been in the hospital—fully demented—and they would be asking him to make decisions he's not qualified to make. But because I had power of attorney, I could make those decisions for him.

The health care directive is the other thing we tell people to have. It states whether you'd want to be kept alive on life support or have the plug pulled. That's a personal choice. If you decide to keep going, you have got to have the funds to take care of that because it can really deplete your savings. Making that decision in advance takes the burden off your family to choose for you.

As I mentioned before, I am an advocate of long-term care insurance, but there are a lot of policies out there that I just don't like. It seems more policies used to provide a lifetime benefit. Now, traditional long-term care policies typically only pay a limited amount, and when the pool is depleted, that's it.

A downside of long-term care policies is that they're a health insurance product from private companies, meaning that the insurance companies have the right to adjust your costs, as needed. You might get a 3 to 5 percent increase in the cost of your policy even though your benefits don't change. They can send out letters saying you can keep your current benefits at a higher cost, or you can keep the cost with less benefits. I have a problem with that because, by the time you get to seventy-five to eighty-five years old, the rates might be so high that many people get out because they can't afford them. They have a fixed income, and if they only have $2,000 a month, they can't afford it.

The problem is long-term care companies are taking a beating on claims. They raise their rates to cover costs. There is a tremendous need to cover their risks for clients. People are living longer now than they used to because of advances in medical sciences. The things that used to kill people aren't anymore.

So, is a long-term care insurance policy worth it? There are some products out there that, I think, are fantastic. For example, the State Life One America long-term care plan is built on a life insurance policy chassis that keep rates locked in for life with an unlimited pool.

Long-term care costs might be a real problem for many and should be addressed in your retirement income planning because there are products that provide solutions to help alleviate, not eliminate, your overall cost.

So, when you retire, what will you do? Do you have a family member that can help take care of you? That's something to consider, because like it or not, it's a real issue.

Pension Distribution

Pensions have become pretty uncommon, but if you're fortunate enough to have one, you have two ways of taking your distribution. What is your wisest way of doing it?

1. You can transfer it over into your own personal IRA, and then you manage it. You eventually will take your required minimum distributions, starting at age seventy-three. This may help you manage that money a little bit better.

2. You can leave your money in the pension. Let's say your pension is paying $5,000 a month. You can choose to receive that full amount, and when you die, the pension dies with you. Or if you're married, you can set it up so that you only receive a reduced amount, say, $4,000 a month. Then when you die, your spouse will continue to receive $2,000 monthly payouts as long as they live. I don't think that's always the best option but it's the one I see more people make. You're giving up $1,000 a month so that your spouse will continue to receive $2,000 a month of taxable income for as long as they live.

   If you also already have a well-structured, well-designed life insurance policy, then you might be paying less than $1,000 a month for that. When you pass away, your spouse will get the same income stream as a survivor benefit, tax-free. And, if your spouse should die before you, then you are still stuck with $4,000 a month—you still miss out on your extra $1,000 a month.

So, we show people that by simply doing some future strategizing and potentially having well-structured life insurance, you can help maximize the full amount.

I encourage people to talk about and plan strategies for retirement so that when you get to that point, you will know what your best options are.

CHAPTER 9

How to Choose a Financial and Insurance Professional

For a moment, I want to turn the tables on you, the reader, and I want to ask what you are looking for in a financial professional.

You are a consumer. What is it you look for when you want someone to work for you?

Do you go with your gut? Someone who is trustworthy? Someone who answers all your questions and doesn't laugh at what you don't know?

Is that enough?

Do you go by friends' recommendations?

I had this discussion with my son. He likes to give clients a lot of technical information. But I think it is more than that. I believe it's not how much you know, but how much you care. A client wants to know you are knowledgeable, but also that you can empathize, rather than sympathize. If you can understand and feel the concerns and pains they have in some areas, they will sense that. You must be willing to understand where a client is coming from and put them at ease.

People often say I make it easy for them to understand.

What is it that you feel when you go see somebody for the first time?

A lot of stockbrokers or brokerage houses won't deal with an investor unless somebody has a significant amount in assets under management. Anything less than that, they don't get professional attention. I just don't agree with that.

Some brokers will say they deal with bigger clients, and they don't give attention to somebody without at least$500,000. Most people don't have that much money themselves.

We try to put people at ease when they come in to see us. Whatever your questions are, we will answer them. We want to take care of you.

If you have $20,000, we will help you manage it because if it is important to you, it is important to us—the same goes for our clients with $20 million.

When people come in to see us, I try to listen between the lines. If there is friction, I try to balance what the husband is saying with what the wife is saying. I can usually figure out quickly where the friction is. You can pick up on certain things that people are saying and find a problem that maybe they are even unaware of. They may even be the problem themselves.

We have one of those situations right now, where you can only help the clients so much, and then you kind of wash your hands because they keep getting in debt. I suggest to them what to do, but they don't do it. They want me to come back and fix it again. Eventually, I will say, "You are the problem and until you fix yourself, I can't help you."

I make it clear to people that come to our seminars that when you come in for a visit, you are going to determine pretty quickly if you like me or not.

If you don't like me, that's fine. There is no obligation to do business with me at all. I want to work with nice people. We have a strict rule around here: we look out for the client's best interest first.

I can't tell you the number of people we have helped and didn't get paid a dime. And I'm fine with that. The way I look at it, the good Lord will take care of me somewhere else that I'm not even aware of. I don't worry about it.

I honestly don't look at how much money I am going to make by helping people. What I get out of it is that I feel good. I go home at night, and I ask myself if I had a good day. Well, did I make money? I may not have, but if I helped somebody, that in turn will pay dividends down the road somewhere. I've taken care of some clients for over forty years.

The purpose of this book is two-fold. In my mind, it is something to pass down to other family members. From a business standpoint, I want people to read this book and understand not only who I am, but also that this is the passing on of a business and values that goes from one generation to the next.

I believe that you learn from previous generations—from your elders—the things and values that were entrusted to you and that were instilled in your life. That becomes the foundation that you use to build the next generation.

I was blessed to have a great relationship with my parents. Some people didn't, and I say you can learn from that—you don't need to carry the negative forward. You learn from the things that were not good and you don't repeat them. You build on that, and it makes you stronger, not weaker. Why do you honor an individual's weaknesses by being weak yourself? To me, it is about taking the good things and building on those.

I honor my mother and father by passing on the things they taught me because they learned those things from their parents.

I've been successful because of hard work and what was instilled in me and the opportunities that my grandparents gave my dad, and my dad then gave to me. I wasn't born with a silver spoon in my mouth.

People who don't know me think I may have inherited this business from my dad. No, my dad wasn't in this business.

When I started this business, I had one file—it was my first sale. Then, I had a second file. They were in one drawer and would keep falling over. I'd close the drawer and I'd say, "You all, multiply. Make babies."

I started with one file, and I built it up to where I now have a large room full of them. Everything in my office and my home is because of hard work.

I don't take that lightly.

It is important to me to feel somebody's needs, worries, concerns, or excitement and to be so keenly tuned in that you can answer their question before they have even asked it.

If a person comes in and feels intimidated or anxious or feels they are asking stupid questions, it tells me I've got to meet them where they are and make them feel comfortable.

When it comes to making decisions, I get very analytical. I am slow to decide. I want to think things through. A lot of people make snap decisions. I don't. I look at all the angles and the negatives. I look at the downside of doing something and people would get on to me and say I was always focused on the negative. I want to know where the dangers and pitfalls are.

I once worked for a very successful businessman. He told me people would kid him and give him a hard time about taking time to make decisions. But he said, "It's a gift. It is a gift to be able to look at things analytically. It's a gift most people don't have."

What's the Cost?

The Good Lord has provided for me. When you work with me and my team, we are transparent about how we are compensated for our time and efforts.

If you have been my client and I have proven my worth to you, and you value our relationship, then refer me to people like yourself.

A lot of people, when they come into our office, think they need to bring a ton of money. I will be honest, I don't put a minimum amount on what people need to bring in. I don't care. We are problem solvers.

I don't look down my nose at anyone because $100,000 to him may feel like a lot more money than it does to the $20 million guy.

I remember when I was twenty-one, I got on the elevator at the Lamar Life Insurance Company. The president of the company was on the elevator along with Sam, the manager of the company supply room. I walked in. They both put their hands out to shake my hand.

I had a dilemma. Whose hand do you shake first? Most people might reach out and shake the president's hand first.

I shook Sam's hand first. I then reached over and shook the president's hand, second.

He never had a problem with that.

If I had shook the president's hand first, it would have just flattered his ego. But it meant more to Sam. It made him feel good.

My point is, when clients come in, I don't care how much money you have. If I can help you, I will help.

CHAPTER 10

The Hunt

I keep a journal every time I go out on a hunt. I have been doing that since the 1970s. I write down all my thoughts, every time we go out.

Sometimes I write about being grateful or thankful.

Other times it might be about the experiences I have with my son or a friend.

I have been blessed to hunt in some very good places.

I wear the same hat I've been wearing since the early 1980s, a Stetson hat.

When I hunt, I like to figure out wildlife patterns and then I like to see if I can figure out the deer patterns and it becomes a competition between me and the deer.

It is a goal. Almost every deer I have gone after, I have been able to harvest.

But it can sometimes take years to get to know an area—and to study the patterns and bedding areas. It is a cat-and-mouse game you play.

How Hunting Affects My Business

I see hunting as a goal.

If you've read this far, you now know this: trying to achieve a goal is fun for me. It may take a year or two before I get the specific animal I'm after.

A lot of my best thoughts are sometimes out in a tree stand. It's where I can be creative.

It is easy to work all the time. But when you work all the time, you can easily get distracted and overwhelmed. And when you do, you can lose creativity.

I remember one time when I hunted up in Illinois, I was sitting in a stand and I thought of an opportunity for a client about a problem he had and it hit me how we could save him $34,000 a year.

I thought of something that would work. A lot of times, those types of thoughts come from getting away and reformatting my mind. It is about decompressing yourself and learning to relax.

I learned from another hunter that—because of my personality—I'm in the attack mode. He told me that the deer would sense that threat.

You are in the deer's world; they are not in yours. And when you sit in a tree, you need to sit back and just disappear. Melt into the tree and just soak it up. Use your senses.

Listen for the first sounds of the morning—a bird's call, the whispers of the wind, the rustle of leaves. Watch for the first shooting rays of the sun. Smell the woods, the musty smells of earth. Watch for other wildlife and observe what they do as they walk by.

As a result, you'll see more deer because they do not sense a threat in the woods. When I do that, I can feel the weight of the world being lifted from my shoulders.

I can relax. No one is pulling or tugging at me. I feel peace in nature. It is okay to relax and free your mind of all the clutter.

When you can do that, you can think freely and creatively.

Touching the Face of God

When I go to Colorado, I sit on a certain ridge—it's named Bobby Dye Ridge. It's near Alamosa, Colorado, near the Great Sand Dunes National Park.

I have always wanted to see something from my grandfather's eyes—how things may have looked in the 1800s and early 1900s. Things he may have seen. Trees will grow and eventually fall. Houses will be built and then, decay. But the mountains are more ever-lasting.

I took some of my father's ashes up there. Someday, I will take my mother's ashes, and someday, my family will take my ashes up there.

When I sit on that rock, I know that most of my grandchildren and great-grandchildren will eventually be able to do the same; and see the same mountain range I am seeing.

It is total peace.

It was there I saw a lone coyote. Another time, a herd of elk came out into the meadow. I've seen bison and an eagle.

It's just me and nature.

There are no phone calls, emails, no interruptions.

I like to golf. But truly, hunting—or rather, just being out in nature—is where I find peace. And that is why I like to be out in nature, go by my instincts, and figure things out.

It comes back to never forgetting where you came from, honoring the past and preparing for the future.

I don't want my family's legacy to get diluted. As the title of this book suggests, I was taught to remember who you are and where you came from.

If you recall, at my high school graduation, my grandparents gave me two $1 bills, which I've kept because I know what those dollar bills symbolize.

Your legacy can sometimes get diluted over time with success. If you are successful and you grow, you might forget who did the groundwork to get you where you are today.

Most likely, one of your ancestors had to do the groundwork. Somebody had to live in a tool shed. Somebody had to farm. Somebody had to pick that cotton by hand. Somebody had to do the work to help you get to where you are today.

So, I encourage you to not forget where you came from.

Don't forget who you are—your job in this generation is to take your legacy forward to another level.

CHAPTER 11

The Wedding

I often wondered why people cry at their child's weddings, especially when it is a time of celebration.

I suppose it is an acknowledgment of a change of life. It's seeing someone turn from a child to a spouse. It's a happy occasion.

It represents the end of one phase of life and the beginning of a new time of life.

Think of a dream day. For me, it was my daughter's wedding day.

The weather couldn't have been prettier.

The band was phenomenal.

But it was when Laura, my daughter, went over to my mother and acknowledged her love and respect with a kiss on the cheek that made me understand why people cry at weddings!

My mother never wanted the spotlight. But she did like respect, appreciation, and being loved, which she definitely deserved.

What is a moment like that worth?

There is no price tag to put on something like that.

Just a few weeks later, my mother died.

That wedding was perfect.

The moment was perfect.

It was a privilege to have the money available to finance that celebration. I'm thankful I could see the joy in my daughter's eyes and see how much fun she was having. Her husband was so appreciative and everybody who attended came and enjoyed the time.

It took me more than thirty years of saving, but the blessing of it was knowing the years of hard work, scrounging, scrapping to get by, and then having the opportunity to do that for such a large group of people.

I told my wife it was one of the best days of my life.

Our daughter, Laura, is reserved, quiet, and doesn't have to have things over the top. It was beyond her expectations and that's what made every penny spent worth it to me.

I have no regrets.

This is a memory our family will have for the rest of their lives. She will take this memory with her to her grave. She will have this long after I'm gone—whereas the money you save disappears after you are gone.

One of my best friends, Ed Lawler, at the wedding came up to me and pulled me aside and said, "Spence Dye would be so proud, right now."

That meant a lot to me. I took it as a sign of encouragement. My dad would have been blown away.

One side of you hurts a bit because I sure wish he was here to enjoy it. But I am thankful on the other side that my mother was there, joyful that God provided me with opportunities to succeed, and gave me encouragement to succeed.

Life Goes On

Ironically, my nephew and his wife had their first son the night before the wedding. The little boy's name is Spence Dye. They named the baby after my father.

There were four generations of Dye family members at the wedding. When I gave my talk at the rehearsal dinner, I said I wanted to talk with the dads in attendance, more specifically the dads of little girls.

Little boys are great, but you can throw them in the backyard and don't need to worry about them. They are going to be fine.

But little girls are something special to a dad. No matter how much you girls think you know about your father's love for you, you don't any idea how important you are to your dad.

After the wedding, some men came up to me—and some women—who told me how they appreciated hearing that. Most dads are not verbal about the place in their hearts for their daughters. But they feel it, I can promise you that.

A Message to My Daughter

All of us in the family had nervous jitters before the wedding. I took a few days off before. I told my daughter that all the hard work had been done and she should just soak in the good. The moment will be done and gone before you know it. Enjoy it.

Soak in the moment and don't get caught up in all the minutiae. Don't get caught up in the distractions that will come. Keep your head clear. Just enjoy, you have worked hard for this.

Don't let people come in at the last moment and steal your joy. Don't let Satan get in there and ruin what is such a glorious moment and that which you do before the Lord.

You are making a vow before the Lord with your spouse— don't let Satan steal your joy with distractions.

Maybe the flowers aren't perfect or there is a cloud in the sky. Don't look for the negatives. Focus on the positives. Slow down and enjoy. Keep your eyes on the prize and what you are achieving.

Don't let other people who don't think the same way become your disturbance. I don't want to associate with people like that because they don't bring any value.

It all comes back to setting goals.

Keep Your Eye on the Prize

So now, how do you come back from the mountain top after something like that?

I tried to clear my head and get back into the routine of things. We still had an end-of-the-year goal to meet, but it puts things in perspective. If we can make one or two good things happen, we are going to be very, very close.

If we achieve our business goals, that's great. If we come up a little shorter, it just means it was the perfect goal that pushed me for 365 days. But when you wake up the next morning and it is January 1, we start the process all over again.

What is your goal?

The important thing is to keep life in perspective. This is a time to reflect on being thankful—how proud I am to be a father, but also to know how proud my father would have been. My daughter's wedding would have exceeded his expectations.

It comes back to the fact that I get to do this.

When I began to think of it in those terms, it changed my whole perspective. It's not about "I have to do this," but rather, "I get to do this."

It is a privilege. And that is what I have focused on. It is a privilege to serve.

I enjoy doing things for people that are unexpected. I don't like to do things that are expected.

That's it in a nutshell.

As I close this chapter, I cannot properly convey the look on my mother's face after my daughter walked away. It was complete happiness and a feeling of being honored, loved, and respected.

It was perhaps the greatest gift my mother had ever received.

As a son and a dad, I cannot put a price on how great a gift it was. But it made every penny I spent worth it.

As I said earlier in this book, I could never pay back to my mother everything she did for me. But my daughter made me a lot closer.

I am privileged to have been able to give them the best on this wedding day.

No regrets.

Very blessed.

My daughter's best day and my mom's best day were the same day.

I am one lucky guy!

The Next Generation Steps Forward

By Gary Dye

EDITOR'S NOTE: Gary Dye represents the third generation of Dye family members who have worked in the public. Gary became licensed as an insurance producer in 2014, while also completing a master's degree in business administration at the University of Mississippi. He joined Dye Resource Management, LLC in April 2018, where he is a registered advisor .

I n business school, you are taught that the goal of any business is to provide a service or product that solves a problem or makes an improvement. To grow a business, you must increase your efficiency in creating the service or product. Both of these statements are true and should be reflected upon in the decision-making process, but where textbooks fail (and always will) is teaching the student the human element of a business.

In every successful business venture, there is a highly motivated, determined person, who finds self-value in the service or product they deliver. Examples exist in nearly every sustainable business.

This person establishes the soul of the business, the heartbeat of it. Without this factor of human nature, the business eventually ceases to exist.

It is worth studying and thinking about.

As Dye Resource Management, LLC grows and looks toward the future, it is critically important that we remember where we came from, what motivates us, and who we are as a family. These characteristics define our reputation as a business, and they dictate how a customer perceives us.

When I reflect on Grampaw's memoirs, I am awestruck at the difficult living conditions. Despite those conditions, he sought opportunity. He was always an optimist. He found opportunities where most people would see stagnation. This attitude came naturally and gave him the ability to find the tiniest diamonds in the thickest of rough, and he would polish those diamonds into better opportunities throughout his life.

Throughout his memoir, I pay special attention to the people that gave Grampaw opportunities. They could have easily seen a poor, skinny, hillbilly kid from nowhere and looked the other way, but that is not what happened. They showed him respect, and I have zero doubt in my mind that potential others saw in him inspired him and elevated him.

He was never motivated by greed. Did he want a nice car, home, to play unlimited rounds of golf? Sure, but to desire these things does not make one greedy. These things are what he considered financial success to look like, and he achieved it. He had many opportunities to make substantially more money, but that was not important. If others respected him, if he felt like he was helping others in need, and as long as he was loving his family, he was deeply satisfied.

That deep satisfaction made him the wealthiest man on Earth in my opinion, not in the checking account, but in his soul.

I also reflect on my dad's journey in this business, which is congruent with how he has lived his life. Loyal to family and faith, giving esteem to all people in his personal interactions regardless of social class, a doggedness to succeed in every endeavor, and pedestal of respect for the people that helped him along the way.

As I examine the core of Dye Resource Management, LLC., the diamonds to success begin to sparkle brilliantly from the rough.

Both my father's and grandfather's stories have the same common themes, attitudes, and core motivators.

This is the roadmap that determines the future of our interactions with retirees.

Challenges will continue to face us. They will come from all sides, from clients, from a need to produce more, from internal business decisions to personal challenges.

So, our goal is to maintain a positive attitude.

And never overlook the tiny diamonds in the rough.

Those small positives in life lead to great opportunities. Challenges present opportunities to express the highest levels of creativity and allow the client to see how much you care.

In this company, we have no minimum case sizes.

Our philosophy is simply this: if the Lord places one of his children in front of us, and we are asked to help, and we have the ability to help, then the case is big enough for us.

This goes back to showing everyone respect, regardless of social class.

We now have the obligation to look for opportunities to help people.

The business financial sheets cannot support this, if we seek to provide value to everyone then I am confident that the Lord will provide and continue to use us to give help to His people.

Our goal is also to teach people what success looks like.

Sure, there are financial aspects to success, but many people are left wanting more money. We help people to live relatively free of economic considerations by helping create financial independence.

We ask people to determine what is most important to them in life, and often their human nature will provide remarkably similar answers (family, children, health, work, peace in knowing what my future looks like). These are the things we preserve. We help clients focus more on things they value most.

Life is often about the phase we are going through in the moment.

Perhaps you are just facing the beginnings of your adult career path. Maybe you are midway along. Or, just now looking at retirement.

Whatever stage of life you are in, our hope is that you have enjoyed reading this book.

You have become acquainted with us.

Thank you for giving us your time.

If you want to know more, feel free to follow us at dyefinancial.net, or give us a call at 601-977-4004.

Going forward, now and for as long as I'm around, the goals of Dye Resource Management, LLC will be reflective of the previously listed traits.

Faces may change and get older. There might even be new faces from time to time, but you must always feel that you are getting our best, you are being esteemed and regarded as family, and that your personal wealth is being preserved for you now and in the future for ones you love.

If you and I have never met, then I look forward to you coming into the office one of these days.

If this book resonated with you, then we already know one another, and we will greet one another as old friends. If you are already a client, then you already know that you are welcome to visit anytime, and you know how much we appreciate your faith in us .

About the Author

BOBBY DYE
Owner, Dye Resource Management, LLC

Since entering the insurance industry in 1981, Bobby has been helping families and individuals pursue financial success by building strategies for retirement income. He proudly serves his clients with trusted, valuable, and unbiased financial guidance. Bobby holds his life and health insurance licenses in various states throughout the country to better serve his clients.

Bobby earned his bachelor's degree in business at the University of Mississippi, where he also played football.

Outside the office, he spends his time golfing, bowhunting, fishing, and riding his motorcycle. A resident of the Jackson area for close to fifty years, Bobby and his wife, Darnell, along with their beloved dog, Molly, currently live in Madison. They have two children: Laura, who is married to Andrew, is an interior designer in Virginia; and Gary, who is married to Shelby, started working alongside his father in 2018.